Who this book is for

If you are starting out in business, own your business, are a CEO or are a manager within a business, then this book is for you.

Every aspect and every chapter of Diary of a Fortune Hunter is relevant to a one person business or a multi-national because the lessons and learning are the same, no matter what size you are. We all have to watch the profit and grow the business at the same time and this is the spirit of the book, to do exactly that.

If you are a business owner or a CEO then the lessons here have captured 21 years of being in business and building a multi-million pound one organically through many trials and errors, and all self taught.

If you are a manager then each chapter will open your eyes on how to be a far better one and drive your area of the business upwards, which will ultimately bring with it its rewards.

This book is for you if you want to really get under the skin of profitability and how to create it in your business; it is a very different way of looking at your business.

This is not a 'How To' book; it is quirky and very real from real life experiences from over two decades.

"So what you're saying is that we've been defunct and out of business for over two years and you've just been waiting for the right time to tell me?"

Diary of a Fortune Hunter

A week-by-week guide to building your
multi-million pound entrepreneurial empire

By Lyndon Wood

Published by
Filament Publishing Ltd
16 Croydon Road, Waddon
Croydon, Surrey CR0 4PA

Telephone: +44 (0) 208 688 2598
email: info@filamentpublishing.com

www.filamentpublishing.com

ISBN 978-1-908691-12-5

© 2012 Lyndon Wood

Lyndon Wood asserts the right to be identified as the author
of this work in accordance with the Designs and Patents Act 1988

Printed by the Berforts Group - Stevenage and Hastings

Designed by Clare Clarke - Evoke Graphic Design

I would like to dedicate this book to my lovely wife, Shirley Ann, and my four children, Maddelena, Ayeshia, Logan and Dior.

It takes the whole family to support you when you are growing a business, small or large, and mine have done me very proud. Hopefully my little ones will follow in the footsteps of their Dad and make a success out of whatever they choose to do.

xxx

Acknowledgements

Sian, my Managing Director at Moorhouse Group, with whom I have debated and discussed and who has put into practice many of the chapters in this book.

I would like to acknowledge all of the people that work for me now and that have done so in the past who have allowed me to learn and grow my skills through trial and error whilst growing the businesses, whereby all the important bits have now been documented in this book.

Thank you.

Lyndon

Contents

Autumn - Troubleshooting — **207**

Follow me on twitter@lyndonx

Visit www.diaryofafortunehunter.com
for more information and free downloads

Introduction

There are literally hundreds of 'How To' books on becoming an entrepreneur. They'll tell you how to do just about everything from registering for VAT, to dealing with banks, to how to pitch to clients. In fact, they will tell you pretty much anything except one important thing. How to make money. And lots of it.

Everyone is a fortune hunter. We are all chasing those elusive millions, the rich man's or woman's lifestyle, the flash car, the home in the sun and the grand mansion. The difference is, few people will ever realise that dream.

I have realised that dream. I founded and own Moorhouse Group, Constructaquote.com, Moorlife and L & S Investments, and at the time of writing this, employ more than 140 people and turn over tens of millions of pounds in insurance premiums. I also have a portfolio of property rentals. I have accumulated a total net worth of circa £16m plus and along the way, I've collected several great cars, have fantastic houses in Wales and in Marbella, Spain. In all, I have enough money to live a pretty comfortable life. I am not bragging, that's not my style. I am simply showing that I did what I set out to do.

When I started out, I didn't want to be 'in insurance', in fact, I knew pretty much nothing about the market. I just knew that I wanted to make my fortune. That was my aim. How I did it really did not matter.

I didn't start off with too many advantages in life or a string of qualifications from top notch academic institutions. In fact, it would be fair to say I didn't have any advantages at all. Some of this was down to circumstance - my parents were not wealthy and split when I was one -

and some was to do with my own stubborn, independent streak. I hated school and could never really get on with it. I'd rather have gone out to train all day in martial arts, which was a real passion of mine. So at the age of 14-years-old, I walked out of the school gates and never really went back.

It would be fair to say I was a pretty shy and withdrawn kid. Despite my passion for martial arts, I would never say boo to anyone. I even ended up sleeping in my rust bucket of a car for a while in minus four degrees over an unjustified parental disagreement over my new girlfriend who turned out to be my first wife. Somehow, at 19-years-old, I found myself living in sin, owning a tiny house and working in a commission-only job selling insurance. Then one day, I had one of those light bulb moments.

"Why don't I do this for myself?" I thought. "What is the point of doing all this work when someone else gets all the benefit and I get a tiny bit of commission? With a bit of hard work, I am sure I could make millions."

I gave up my job and started selling insurance for myself. Now, if you were a business advisor back then, your eyes would have raised through the roof. I had just turned 19-years-old; I had no qualifications and no real experience. Plus, I had £6,000 of mortgage arrears to my name and £4,000 of other debts. To cap it all, the year was 1990, and the UK was at the start of a recession, mortgage rates were 15 per cent and the economic outlook could not have been bleaker.

None of this really bothered me. I just knew I wanted to make my fortune and thought I had better get on with making it happen. I quickly discovered that I faced a real obstacle in dealing with the various insurance companies. Well, I say an obstacle; actually they wouldn't deal with me at all. In those days, everything had to go via an agency and as I didn't have one, I was persona non grata. The only way I could get around this was to place any business I could get with two established brokers, who would pay me commission for the lead.

It wasn't an ideal situation, because I was effectively working for commission once again albeit under my own trade name, but hey, beggars can't be choosers and I worked hard to build up my business.

I didn't mind the hard work. I always knew why I was doing it. In those early days, when I was earning just £100 a week, I can vividly recall thinking that if I ever made it to the dizzying heights of earning £1,000 a month; I would be in God's pocket! Then, of course, by the time I made it to £1,000 a month, I had already started to think about £2,000 and then £4,000. I never stopped setting myself challenges and never stopped believing that I could achieve that fortune.

In some ways, my timing was right (although that was mostly by default than by design I may add), in that it was a good market for insurance when I started out and after a while brokers started sending me business too. Over the next few years, I built up a nice little business and even started employing people to help me. I was starting to feel pretty good about things.

I'd like to say it was plain sailing after that and that five employees turned into 10, then 20 and then 40; profits doubled every year; and I was a millionaire by the time I was 27. And a multi-millionaire by the time I was 30. But it wasn't plain sailing. In fact, running my own business has been a bit of a roller coaster ride during which I have come close to losing everything twice. The terrorist attacks of September 11 2001 hit my industry pretty hard, and I will tell you more about my strategy to get through that crisis later in this book. I also had to find my way through various archaic practices in my industry, sheer snobbery from some of the big players, and evermore stringent rules from industry regulators. Dealing with a growing team has always been a real bugbear to me over the years too, and I have had to learn various strategies to drive the best performance and motivate the people that have helped me on the way to success.

Over the years though, I have learned a lot about what works - and what doesn't - when you set up and run your own show with a view to making your fortune. As my business has grown and prospered, I have used these learnings to help other entrepreneurs and business owners. I always try to respond to calls for help from people running small businesses and give people my time when I can. I have even become an investor in a number of firms, helping them both financially and with advice.

Now, 21 years after I first went it alone in my quest for a fortune, I thought it would be a good time to set down what I have learned over this time and help other fortune hunters. Diary of a Fortune Hunter is not a guide through the vagaries of the insurance market though. It is a week-by-week planner which will help you in any business you chose, whether you are selling widgets, or wing nuts. I decided to steer away from the usual dry book format of 'how to run your business', with lengthy turgid chapters on process, because I wanted this diary to be a practical and interesting reference book. I have written this book with the busy entrepreneur in mind. My own experiences from school have shown me how important it is to engage your reader in the subject and then keep their interest - or there is little point bothering. School never engaged me enough; hence I left at the age of 14.

Diary of a Fortune Hunter is therefore as quirky and unconventional as I am, but this approach has not done me any harm and could well help you. It is broken down as a 52-week diary planner, covering topics as diverse as getting the most out of social media, to dealing with time thieves (people who constantly want to steal your time and divert you from your true purpose). There is advice on everything from dealing with advisors, to employees, to the thorny issue of scaling up your business fast. I have further sub-divided it into seasons, to reflect the journey of an entrepreneur through the various stages of the process, from starting the business (spring), building it up (summer), dealing with any problems (autumn), and then selling up and realising your fortune (winter).

Although it starts at the beginning with tips on how to set your business up, and ends at the end, discussing how to sell the firm, it does not have to be read sequentially. It's perfectly fine to dip in and dip out of the diary, to find the information you need. You choose - it is your fortune that you are hunting.

I've made plenty of mistakes along the way, but I have had my fair share of breakthroughs and triumphs too. My golden rule has always been that, as long as those breakthroughs exceed the disasters, you should do OK, as I have. If my experience can help another fortune hunter in any small way, I will be delighted.

Good luck!

SPRING

Taking the plunge to start a business can be the most scary, yet exhilarating, experience there is.

At any one time there will be hundreds of questions buzzing around your head and probably a fair smattering of doubts too. Worse still, your 'to do' list will stretch far into the distance. The Spring section of this diary will attempt to unravel the confusion, ignore the stuff you really don't need to worry about and help you concentrate on the few, vitally important, steps that are needed to get your business off the ground and get you on the way to making your fortune.

Let's get started!

Speed beats perfection

Scribble your stuff here

Week 1

Do you have what it takes to be a fortune hunter?

When I started my insurance business at the age of 19-years-old, the odds were stacked against me. I had no money, I had left school at 14 with no qualifications, I had no real support from my family and didn't know anything about insurance. (Of course I was just 19, so what the hell did I know about anything?) Oh, and I was launching smack, bang, into the teeth of a recession. Did this put me off? Not a bit of it. I knew I was going to make my fortune and was prepared to do anything to get it.

People start their own businesses for many reasons. For some, it is an economic necessity after losing their paid jobs and being unable to find employment elsewhere. For others, it is down to a deeply felt desire to be masters of their own destiny. A few want the big money and know that it is only by running their own show that they will realise the fortune they desire.

It is this third group that this diary is primarily concerned with, so it might be useful to start off by setting you a test to see if you have what it takes to be a bona fide fortune hunter.

Look at the following qualities of a fortune hunter and answer honestly which ones you think you already possess:

1. Are you impatient?

Being impatient is often seen as a negative quality, but for a fortune hunter it is one of the best attributes you can have. Sitting back and waiting for things to come to you is for losers. If you don't demand that things happen the day before yesterday, your business can and will drift. Business does not just happen. You have to make it happen. Be impatient and proud of it.

2. Do you have a vision?

When I first started, my vision was that I just wanted to earn £100 per week, which seemed a fortune to me then. Then, once I achieved that (easily, I may add) I moved the goalposts and increased my goals. All fortune hunters should set out how much they want to make and by when. Then, they should look at their business and ask; is it the right business, with the right products, to fulfil that vision? If you have vision, it will enable you to see what others don't and it will encourage you to think outside the box. Remind yourself of that vision every day.

3. Can you do a deal?

What separates good, profitable, businesses from average ones is your ability to do a deal. The key is to be fluid in your thoughts whilst discussing a deal and, of course, knowing when to walk away. Your skills in negotiation will improve as you grow with the business, but you should always be trying to get better at it. You should, for example, make it your goal to close as many deals as possible during meetings, so you walk out with an order and don't leave anything open for a competitor or a change of mind.

4. Do you always spot an opportunity?

Not everyone can spot an opportunity, even when it is staring them in the face. Are you the sort of person who, when out at an event or dinner, is constantly listening out for signs of needs, struggles or frustrations? If you are not readily alert to these potential opportunities, you can bet some other fortune hunter will be.

5. Can you be both fair and firm?

To be a successful fortune hunter, you will have to pull off the balancing act of being both fair and firm with both customers and employees. Everyone wants to believe they are being treated well and are getting the best deal, but you also have to make your money too. The trick is to treat your team, customers and other businesses how you would like to be treated. You will win respect and people will want to work with you.

6. Can you cut through the crap?

A canny fortune hunter will have the ability to not get distracted by events and activities that are not productive and get straight to the main point of what really matters. Others will constantly try to pull you off track (either intentionally or unintentionally) and it is up to you to get them back in line and on to the subject in hand.

7. Can you keep it simple?

Most human beings seem to naturally gravitate towards the view that the more complex something is, the better it will work. This could not be further from the truth. Simplicity rules. If you do not have the ability to cut to the chase and make things simple, you will tie yourself and your business up in time-wasting knots.

8. Do you know your numbers?

Your quest to become a fortune hunter is a non-starter if you are not good with figures. You do not have to be an accountant, but you do need a good, solid understanding of what you buy and sell at, as well as of your central costs, such as rent, rates and salaries. You should also know inside out what makes your highest profit and what makes you the least.

9. Ideas, ideas, ideas.

No business can survive through to the medium and long term without a constant stream of ideas to try and test. You can never have enough ideas. Create an ideas register for yourself, keep a log of all your thoughts (however off the wall) and encourage others to add to the list too. Not all of the ideas will work, but the important thing is to have a constant stream to choose from to keep your business fresh.

10. Do you have the mental toughness?

Becoming a successful fortune hunter is not easy. You will take some knocks along the way and may well meet some cut-throat individuals who would like nothing better than to watch you fall on your face. Similarly, not all your endeavours will succeed. You have to be sure that you are tough enough to withstand this pressure and not give up. If you can do this, you will find the good outweighs the bad many times over.

All of these traits are important in your quest to become a successful fortune hunter, but the final one is perhaps the most pertinent of all. The key to success for every fortune hunter is how they deal with failure. Many so-called entrepreneurs give up after getting a knock-back, but if you want to go for the big money you cannot be one of those people. Remember, nearly every leader of the most successful businesses failed at one point or other. The reason they became so prosperous is that they did not give up.

If you have one outstanding quality, make it the ability to deal with failure and adversity. After that, the rest is easy.

Scribble your stuff here

Week 2

The Next Big Thing - How to come up with great ideas and make them happen

Around five years ago, I had a great idea for a business. It would be an internet based service that would offer consumers who subscribed to my site one fabulous deal a day in the area where they lived. Basically a group buying model, it would require a certain amount of people to buy in for deals such as half off a sushi dinner, or spa treatment, before the discount kicked in. I would split the profits 50/50 with the merchant and everyone would get an unbeatable bargain.

I mapped it all out on my Mac, how I would do it, how it would be financed, where I would go to get these great deals and so on. It looked perfect. This is the business that will change the way people bought off the internet the world over, I thought.

Except that idea stayed firmly locked in my Mac. That was as far as it went. It was left to Groupon to devise a business model very similar to my idea (and not connected, I hasten to add) and make it into a business. Groupon changed the world of internet selling and created a $13bn value, not me.

It makes me sick as a parrot to think about it now. Not because I begrudge Groupon their success. They deserve every bit of it. They have built a great little business because the young CEO Andrew Mason got off his backside and made it happen. No, what sickens me is I fell into the trap of every wannabe, yet failed, entrepreneur. These are the people who have amazing and innovative ideas - and then do precisely zip about them.

There is one of these characters on every street. They'll invariably be employed by someone else while constantly muttering about what 'could have been' until the day they go to the grave, taking with them their 'great idea'.

In my defence, I had at least gone as far as mapping out a credible business plan. Most people don't even get that far. Plus, I was already running a number of other entrepreneurial ventures in the insurance arena, so I was pre-occupied with building those. But, yeah, OK, that was the one that got away.

The point of raising this sorry tale is to show that although we all have ideas, it is what you do with them that counts. And, while I failed to act on this occasion, I always have a constant stream of ideas on the go, in various stages of development, trial and expansion. I am not going to make the same mistake twice. That really would be stupid.

True fortune hunters do not begin a business, then sit back and watch the profits roll in. They are constantly coming up with new ideas on how to make things faster, better, bigger. Then, they make them happen. Because, as I found, a world-beating idea has to be released from your computer in order to be turned into cold, hard cash.

So, how do you keep a steady stream of ideas to fuel your fortune hunting ambitions? Well, first of all, it helps to set yourself a target. Like most entrepreneurs, I don't like routine, but in this case I make an exception. My personal target is for one good, new business idea a month. I'll come up with more if I can too.

Where do I get these ideas from? Anywhere and everywhere. My goal is to be in constant communication with people from a variety of industries and sectors. I don't stick to my comfort zone of insurance. There would be no point. I want to know where else there are gaps and I have an unrivalled thirst for knowledge.

Talking to people *will* trigger ideas. If it doesn't, you are not listening properly.

Then, once I have an idea, I write it down. I have a file on the desktop of my Mac marked 'ideas library' and whenever I have one, I add it to the list.

If one of the ideas looks good, I will go on and work up the financials around it. If I am just not quite sure, I leave it on the list anyway. Sometimes a scheme might not look good today, but in a few months' time it might be just right. Similarly, one light bulb moment might not be worth pursuing on its own merits, but when put together with a subsequent one, it will suddenly come alive.

I don't keep them to myself either. I regularly try them out on colleagues, contacts and friends. If I don't get any negative feedback, or rolling of eyes, I can see I might be on to a good thing.

Not every idea is going to be a world beater. But, the great thing is, having a constant stream of ideas keeps your brain active. Often, when you spend a lot of time working on your core business, you get blinkered and insular. It is very easy to become stale and inward looking. Giving the old grey matter a regular workout can be very revealing and if you keep up a regular stream of ideas (however off the wall) you will hit gold.

None of this means I am rushing from pillar to post like a mad man, constantly wasting my time and money on one hare-brained scheme after another. I never get carried away to the point that I am distracted from my day job. Indeed, if I am honest, probably just one out of 20 of my brainwaves make it out of my Mac and into any sort of reality. The point is, I am constantly thinking about what might be the next big thing.

I regularly revisit my list and have a flick through. Many a time I have suddenly thought, yes, that is it. I've got to move on to this one. Then I do.

As the painful illustration at the start of this chapter showed, an idea is only ever an idea. It has to make it off the PC to start making any money. So, if a new business concept warrants fuller attention, I will put some numbers around it. Very often, at this stage, it might emerge that it was not an idea at all. You'll realise when you see the numbers that, while you liked the concept, you don't like it enough to shell out the cash required to make it work and for the return you might get.

If, however, the financials look promising, you have a final test to do. It is a test that only you can do and no one can advise you on.

Ask yourself; do you have the entrepreneurial energy and time that is required to get this project off the ground? Very often, once someone has established one business and understands the gruelling demands involved, the answer to doing it all again is a resounding "No!" That's fine and having started up and run several businesses myself, I can completely understand that. It is always easier the first time, even if you don't quite know what you are doing.

But, if the idea is good enough and deserves an airing, now is the time to summon up your entrepreneurial energy and make it happen. If you don't, you will always regret it.

After my non-start, failed internet deal service, I know that for certain.

Scribble your stuff here

Week 3

Creative Destructive (The Next Big Thing - Part Two…)

A Creative Destructive business is something that has the ability to destroy or re-define an industry. So, if constant innovation and a regular flow of new ideas are key to building a winning portfolio of businesses, a creative destructive venture is absolute nirvana.

A creative destructive business model is one that has the potential to destroy and disrupt an entire industry. Think, for example, of Amazon, which came up with a concept that drove the sales of most books on to the internet. Before that, no one considered that we would do anything else than trot off down to the high street to buy our next read. Or, how low-cost airlines, which offered a bog-standard, no frills, no extras, service, transformed the airline industry. Over the years, as more and more people turn to this budget service, established airlines have been forced to lower their range of services simply to compete.

There are, however, precious few creative destructive ideas. That doesn't stop them, quite rightly, being an object of fascination for avid business watchers. Along the way, it has helped create a few urban myths too. My personal favourite is the everlasting light bulb, which is one of the hoariest myths in business. According to this legend, inventors have regularly come up with designs for this useful household product, but evil-minded light bulb manufacturers have suppressed them to protect the market for their own inferior products. There are equivalent tales for tyres that never wear thin, ladies tights that never ladder and so on. All of them are priceless.

And wrong. (Or are they?!)

However, we mustn't get diverted from the fact that there are still creative destructive ideas out there to be had. As a fellow fortune hunter, this is an area that should be high on the list for your attention.

Creative destructive ideas fall into two camps. The first is to simply spot an industry, any industry, and visualise what that next big leap will be. The second is to look closely at your own sector and predict where the next shocker is coming from. (If you don't think there is any possibility that it is coming from your firm - worry now)

The first of these two is, arguably, a more difficult proposition. You will be looking at areas that you know little about and trying to make credible predictions. But, in a way, that is why it is an easier call too. If you don't know much about a sector, you won't be weighed down by baggage of "We've tried that before and it didn't work". It might now.

Plus, and this is a bit sneaky, don't be afraid to take a leaf out of our mythical light bulb inventor's book. Imagine, if you could come up with an idea that was so threatening to an industry, or even a competitor, that they had to buy you out at the earliest opportunity. You'd be quids in, you wouldn't have the headache of building up the business and you'd be free to get on with your other ventures.

What do I mean by this? Imagine an online discount model such as Living Social, KGB or Groupon (and no, I am not picking on them after the disappointment outlined in the last chapter - it is just an example!). Company A could begin their own internet based deals service. However, Company A could offer the merchant 70, 80 or even 90 per cent of the profits instead of the usual industry standard 50/50 split. The idea being that they would be able to run a profitable business by vastly undercutting the competition through creating a larger volume of punters vying for Company A's deal and coupons.

The result? Either Company A overtakes all the competition and becomes the biggest business in the market or one of the competitors, which is seeing its supply chain being eroded quickly, will buy out Company A tout de suite. Potentially a nice little earner, I am sure you will agree.

It'll obviously take some investment to get an idea like this off the ground, but as every good fortune hunter knows, nothing ventured, nothing gained.

And so to the other side of creative destructive. The Big Idea that will rock your core industry. There will be one, I guarantee it. You may not be able to come up with it straightaway, but the important thing is you are constantly imagining what it might be. If you don't, someone else will.

In my own sector of insurance, there are many instances of this. Direct Line, for example, revolutionised the way people bought car insurance when over 20 years ago; it started encouraging people to buy their cover over the phone, instead of through visiting brokers as they had always done in the past. At their peak they nicked almost 60% of the UK car insurance market. This innovation was followed by the aggregators, such as confused.com and gocompare.com, which market their businesses through big budget TV campaigns largely on price. This again disrupted the entire sector.

The problem with many companies is they get trapped in their own business model. They think; I'm making good money with the current structure, so why change it? Change might destroy your cash cow, cost you money and might not even work anyway. That's just too scary for many businesses.

Look at that the other way though. I'm sure the powers that be at Blockbuster thought all of these things for many years as they happily rented out their videos and DVDs to an eager following of film lovers. There was one of those iconic blue and yellow stores shining brightly on every high street. What could possibly go wrong?

Er, well, some bright spark worked out a better model. Online rentals and Screen Select (which later became LoveFilm) didn't have any great new technology when they started out in 2002; they just worked out that the antiquated distribution system of the Royal Mail suited film lovers better. It wasn't even a huge leap of the imagination either. We'd all known for ages that, before long we'd get movies on our computer, iPads, phones and probably even wristwatches. But, even if Blockbuster thought this, they didn't do a thing about it.

The result? Blockbuster filed chapter 11 in 2010. You may well ask; what were they waiting for?

What happened to Blockbuster could happen to any one of our businesses if you don't constantly imagine what the creative destructive threat is. It is a salient lesson not to be complacent and not to get trapped in your business model. Things always move on. You just have to stay ahead of things.

An important skill for any fortune hunter is to recognise decay and decline, long before it shows up on the balance sheet. Creative destruction should be a vital part of your business strategy. So, start imagining what the next Big Thing is going to be in your sector. Now.

No such thing as "No Time"

Scribble your stuff here

---

www.diaryofafortunehunter.com
Follow me on twitter@lyndonx

Week 4

Getting investment

At the age of 19, when I was in a commission-only job selling insurance and decided I would be better off starting my own company, I never saw getting investment as a problem. If you are a bona fide fortune hunter, there is always a way.

My main challenge was that I couldn't get any insurance company to trade with me. I overcame that by persuading two local brokers to place my business with the insurance companies. Then, every time I received commission on one sale, I'd put it back into the business. For a while I lived on virtually nothing, but gradually the profits started to build up and I was on my way.

No entrepreneur should ever fail to get off the starting blocks because they have not got access to finance. As I write this book, the country is in the grip of yet another downturn and the media is filled with stories of how banks are not lending and small businesses are suffering. This should not be a problem to a fortune hunter.

If you want to start a business and need cash to do it, get off your backside and find some. If you can't even do this, you are not going to succeed.

Even though lending is undoubtedly tight today, there are still a number of options open to you.

The first, and most obvious, port of call is to use your own savings. Sell your car, re-mortgage your house, or put your clutter on eBay. After all, if you are not prepared to use your own cash, how on earth do you think you have the right to persuade anyone to give you theirs?

Alternatively, start a mini business to raise money. Offer to take scrap metal from people's gardens, clean houses, take in ironing, anything. Everyone can sell something to somebody. You just need to have the drive.

If you don't have enough money, or very little as I did, take a leaf out of my book. Do a deal, or sell a small amount of your product, reinvest the money, and then do some more deals. Gradually build up the cash pot towards your eventual goal. Don't be tempted to do as so many do, which is to earn £1,000, then pay themselves £990 and wonder why things are not happening.

There is no shame in this slow burn approach, even if you are in a tearing hurry to earn your fortune. It will make sure you keep on top of your money and in tune with your business. Apart from anything else, companies that saddle themselves with a ton of debt (if they could get finance) really suffer when the economy takes a dive. You can still be ambitious and grow organically as I did.

Some businesses are in a position where they have to invest heavily at the front end. Perhaps they have to have special tools made, or need to buy machinery or stock for a production line. If this is the case, I would consider very carefully how much you really need to make. Could you, for example, buy the equipment second-hand, or rent it? If you have to get outside help on finance, I would always keep the amount you borrow down to the bare minimum. I am a firm believer in winning customers' orders first, then buying the kit after.

Similarly, I would also be very clear about exactly how much you do need in the short, medium and long term. Raising cash is hard work and expensive. A fortune hunter does not want to be in a position of constantly going backwards and forwards to raise additional funding. Areas you should take into account are the start-up costs, i.e. how much you need before you even begin to trade, the cost of fixed assets, working capital for raw materials and whether there might be an investment required in extra capacity if all goes to plan.

As things currently stand, I see little point in approaching banks for a large investment of say £100,000 or more. Most won't even give small businesses the time of day and with no trading record they are simply not interested in the risk, however good your plan.

My preference in this circumstance would be either venture capital firms, or business angels, depending on how great your idea is. Venture capitalists are firms that specifically invest in businesses, although many prefer to deal with companies that already have a track record. Business angels are business people like myself, who provide capital and sometimes advice for start-ups. Many angel investors organise themselves into groups or networks to share research and pool their investment capital.

Both venture capitalists and business angels invest in businesses for a share or stake in the business. You should, therefore, think very carefully how much control you are prepared to give up in your business in return for the cash.

You can, and should, negotiate if and when someone makes you an offer. Just because they say they want a 40 per cent stake in your company in return for a £100,000 investment, does not mean it is their final offer. It helps, of course, if you have some idea of what your company is worth. Simple maths shows that a 40 per cent stake for a £100,000 investment values your company at £250,000. There may well be no clear rationale behind this percentage, so it is well worth the time and money to get a formal valuation from an independent third party.

Whatever happens, you need to put a lot of thought into your business plan and your presentation to would-be investors. You need to get them just as inspired and worked up about your idea as you are.

As a final word, I would caution very strongly against turning to friends or family for investment. It is a slippery slope and 9.9 times out of ten will turn into a dreadful rift (See 'Week 13 - Don't keep things in the family - ever!'). Yes, they probably won't demand extortionate rates or interest, or a seat on the board, but it is a great way to ruin a relationship.

Don't ever let access to finance be the barrier to getting your idea out there. If it is a winner, there are always ways to find money.

Time means nothing in business

Scribble your stuff here

Week 5

Create Customers First

Getting machines, creating a fancy corporate identity, hiring a team of people and buying top-notch computers are all very well. They won't put food on your table though - and they'll drain what little cash you start out with.

One of the most common mistakes of start-ups is they plan everything down to the last degree and get carried away with the kudos of being a new 'entrepreneur'. Somehow though, they forget the most important aspect of running a business.

YOU'VE GOT TO SELL SOMETHING!!

Yes, the only way to start building up that fortune is to think about your customers and what you can sell to them and how, above and beyond everything else.

Don't get carried away by process. What you need to worry about is getting your great idea in front of your customer and getting the money out of their pockets. Apart from anything else, you won't get everything right with your processes in the first place, so it is pointless to waste valuable time before you know what sort of market you have and its scale. Once you've got your customers on board, you can always iron out the back office.

Similarly, no business plan ever survives first contact with the customer. All your carefully made projections and assumptions are just that until a real, living, breathing person tells you what they really want. So, doesn't it make sense to refine your plan first? The quicker you get out there and test your big idea, the quicker you will find out what you really need to do to get that fortune rolling in. It is fine to change your business plan on the hoof, (indeed you probably will, I did and still do) but it is not easy to do if you are too busy choosing which colour floor tiles you want in your corner office.

Sometimes, of course, you need to spend a bit of money first. If you have an internet based business model, for example, you will need the website to function properly before you can start getting your customers to try it in earnest. But don't get so carried away by filling your boots with the most perfect site ever that you run out of cash before a single product is sold.

I confess that this is a lesson I have learned the hard way. When I devised a van insurance website, I invested thousands of pounds and countless hours of blood, sweat and tears into getting the best, whizz-bang site I could get. Though if I say so myself, it looked terrific. When it finally went live after months of painstaking tweaks, I discovered that the online enquiry bit of the site was not working as we had expected and we were missing out on 20 per cent of the leads this super-duper service was creating. I literally had to go back to the drawing board and spent many more hours sorting it out.

I could have saved myself weeks of work if I had gone live sooner and worried about sales first. I could have been correcting the teething problems while reaping the benefit of the sales I could get with my, albeit less than perfect, site.

On other occasions, I have spent a fortune recruiting a team of people in the anticipation of a massive sales surge for some new service or other. Then I have had the frustrating sight of watching them kicking their heels and gossiping around the water cooler when the business takes off far slower than I had expected. I have learned my lesson - sales first, staff and infrastructure second. It doesn't take that long to recruit people or buy desks, so it makes sense to wait until you know they are really needed, rather than wasting money in anticipation.

The key points to remember are:

1. Do not add a ton of back office costs until you have created customers.

2. You don't need lots of lovely promotional banners, spare office space, desks, leaflets and key fobs. Until you know where you are going, this is all a pointless waste of money.

3. Use your PC or Mac to create your own stationery. There are plenty of programs around which will help you do this and come up with some very creative ideas.

4. Spend as little as humanly possible in testing your market and think carefully about how quickly you can get your business to 'go live' so it can be tested in the real world.

5. Do your early PR and marketing by yourself, to save on costs. After all, who knows more about your product than you do?

Never, ever, lose sight of the fact that the most important issue around starting a business is the customer. Without customers, you have no business.

Start-ups that fail, fail because they don't give customers what they want. The founder falls at the first hurdle because he or she forgets why they are doing what they are doing. They get distracted by ego and things that are not important.

Failed start-ups generally blame 'lack of funding', but if you look more closely you will usually find they simply failed to attract customers. They were too slow to get their product or service out in front of people with money to spend.

Constantly remind yourself who the customer is, what needs your product or service will satisfy and why it is the best on the market. Everything else is just superfluous until you get underway.

When others contract, you expand

Scribble your stuff here

www.diaryofafortunehunter.com
Follow me on twitter@lyndonx

Week 6

Tomorrow was Yesterday -
Just get on with it!

If I had £1 for every time someone said to me "I have not got enough time to do that", or "I will look at it next week", or "I could have been a player, but I didn't have the money", I would be a billionaire! My answer to this is always the same; time waits for no one. For an entrepreneur in a hurry, that goes doubly so.

I am a firm believer that if you have a feeling something needs to be done, or there is a big opportunity just waiting to be grabbed, just do it. Now. If you don't, someone will beat you to it.

People may say to me, "Well, it is OK for you; you are clearly a risk taker. I'd rather be cautious and check the numbers thoroughly first." Well, that I may be, but I believe that I am a pragmatic risk taker. I do things in the blind belief that they will work. And, if they don't, I damn well will find a way to make them work.

Apart from anything else, ask yourself one question: if you are not willing to take the risk yourself that your idea might work and are not confident enough in your own ideas and skills, how do you ever expect to convince anyone else to come on board and help you make it happen?

I often return to this subject when a would-be entrepreneur tells me about their amazing idea.

"This one is gonna be a monster," they say.

"Fantastic, get on and do it," I'll reply, being as encouraging as I can.

If they say, "Yeah, well, I'm not sure about quitting my job and I have a mortgage and school fees to pay," then I know they don't stand a chance.

Whenever you try to do anything in business, people will always try to put you off. All the time. They'll come up with platitudes like:

"That sounds fantastic, but take one step at a time."

Or, "Walk before you can run."

Those phrases drive me mad. I always say; what if you think about it another way? If you run while everyone else walks, who will be the ultimate winner? If you do five, six or seven things at a time, while everyone else doggedly sticks to one, think how much your chances of success multiply!

Most real opportunities only strike the once. You have to take advantage of them immediately, or they will pass you by. Very often, I will find myself arriving at the conclusion to say "yes" to an opportunity and then figure out how to make it happen afterwards. That doesn't mean I don't plan diligently and carefully for how to achieve my goal. I just start from the premise that I am going to make it happen and that is a huge boost to making things a reality.

Of course, there are some 'good' risks and some 'bad' risks, but if you want to start your business, grow it and make your fortune, you need to start thinking in terms of taking at least some risks. That means not putting off until tomorrow what you should do today or what you should have done yesterday.

Obviously, for many people, the biggest risk is starting the company in the first place. But, once you get through that one, you will be faced with new risks. Every day.

Examples of some of the 'good risks' you may face include:

- Coming up with an innovative solution to a painful problem with your customer base or supply chain. Yes, it can be high risk if it doesn't work - but doing nothing can be a whole lot worse.

- Replacing your product with a better or cheaper version. The reason so many companies fail is they don't move with the times. Yes, if your current product may be pulling in money, it might seem madness to replace it, but if you don't plan ahead, someone else could well pull the rug from under you and come up with that better product. Always be on the lookout to broaden your opportunity.

- Introducing lots of new products. Every new product you bring in gives you a better chance to stay ahead of your competitors. It will stop you getting stale too.

- Spend money on marketing. Word of mouth and social networking can only go so far. At some point you have to consider spending money to make money.

- Get the best people on board. Hiring the cheapest, or getting family members on board, will backfire (see 'Week 13: Don't keep things in the family - ever!'). If you have a big job to do, surround yourself with the best people who will help you get it done. They may be expensive, but you will get a return many times over.

- Be creative financially. No, I don't mean hire a dodgy accountant! Think about ways of getting more for less. Don't try to solve problems with money; over-funded start-ups invariably crash and burn. Instead, think about how to really stretch your investment.

- Be aggressive with your forecasts. Don't fall into the trap of lowering your forecasts to lessen the risks. You'll just get less achieved, more slowly. Base your forecasts on the opportunity and then ramp it up a notch. I do three forecasts: low ball, achievable and optimistic. Of course, always aim for the optimistic, but base your costs around low ball; you can always add cost to grow profit.

- Lead, don't follow. Don't take comfort in the fact that a dozen other people have tried your idea, so it must be a goer. No, that one is dead in the water. You need a new, untried, yet potentially lucrative idea. That is the way to make the big money.

- Never, ever, ever live in the glory of your business, in the ego trip of being able to say, "Oh, I employ 50 people and have a lovely big office in the city." Forget it and start with making money. The rest will come.

All risks must be measured and managed, but the most important thing is you don't hide behind excuses and platitudes. Apart from anything else, you will be wasting your time if you keep coming up with ideas and then dismissing them because they are too much of a risk.

The level of risk you are prepared to take is directly linked to the level of ambition you have. No risk equals no ambition.

If you are confident of your abilities, ideas and skills, don't be lazy. Just get on with it. You may screw up now and again. In fact, you probably will, just like I did. But, when you win, you will win big. Leave the naysayers to worry about what might have been. They are not in your league.

Microsegment for success

Scribble your stuff here

Week 7

Playing with Personalities (and I don't mean partying with celebs!)

One of the most important things a fortune hunter has to be able to do is to learn how to speak about their business to others. If you can sum up the unique aspects of your service or product in a way that connects with and excites the person on the other side, it is a skill which is worth its weight in gold. I meet so many business owners who fail to describe what they do in a way that would excite me to buy from them. They babble on about this and that, leaving me to ask, "So what do you actually do?" or "What is it you are selling?". That drives me bonkers.

I'm not one for the expression 'elevator pitch', but my experience has shown me the value of being able to make a quick, succinct and helpful summary of what it is you do in a way that will really appeal to the individual you are addressing. In my line of work, people pitch to me every day. As a rule of thumb, it takes me about 10 seconds to work out whether I can do business with this personality or not, and what level of authority they have. It then takes a further 20 or 30 seconds for me to determine what drives this person, how committed they are to their cause and whether they can be of any use to me.

I am constantly amazed how many come to a meeting with me - usually a meeting which could put some business their way and help them deliver to their seniors - and yet they have clearly not given a great deal of thought about it or who they are dealing with. I always think to myself, if I am summing up this person so quickly, why on earth are they not doing the same with me, getting the measure of me as a person and adapting their patter accordingly?

As a business, every meeting you set up is important - or at least it should be or why else are you wasting your valuable time having it? You must give it your all, prepare carefully and capture your audience's attention fast. This does not take much time at all, so please never think you have to spend hours prepping for a meeting. If you do, then you're doing it all wrong.

To give you a head start, I've compiled some do's and don't based on the good and bad pitches made to me.

First and foremost, the do's:

Do - remember that the way you conduct yourself is the way of demonstrating your brand. It can show people that you know more about your market than anyone else, and have ideas which set you apart from all the rest.

Do - prepare. Preparation is the key. It's not enough to know your business inside out either. What is it that will interest and excite the person that you are meeting? What is the best way to convey the vitality behind what it is you do? Plan the meeting in your head before you set off so you don't miss anything vital.

Do - find out who you are speaking to! Always try to speak to the most senior person you can. Failing that, make sure you impress the person you meet so much that they give you access to someone higher up the food chain. The way you will impress them is to appeal to them as an individual.

Do - adapt. Of course, when you get to the meeting you will find that different people will want to hear different things. You will have to be adaptable and able to think on your feet. You must be prepared to quickly switch your language and approach to the person you are addressing. It helps if you have prepared well, but if you have memorised a ready stock of facts and figures, you can use them as and when needed. (Don't, however, try to bedazzle them with everything and everything; you will just succeed in boring or alienating them, or both.)

Do - anticipate what questions you may be asked. And your answers. Politicians do it all the time and it keeps their delivery slick. It's not hard to imagine what your would-be client will ask. If a question catches you off guard, you could well botch the meeting you worked so hard to set up. Plan likely questions and rehearse the answers.

Do - be on time. Better still, be there 10 minutes early. It puts me in a really bad and utterly unreceptive mood if people don't arrive when they said they would. I, like most senior executives, have other things to do.

And the don'ts:

Don't - whatever you do - get flustered and start apologising. Well, not unless you trip over and smash one of their windows or the chairman's prize statue! If you do feel intimidated, remind yourself that most people work for someone else and have pressures of their own to deal with. If you are the guy or girl who is bright enough to give them a solution that will transform their business, they are going to get the credit for it. By being there that day, you may well have turned their fortunes.

Don't - ever get so intimidated by the people you are sitting across the table from that you forget why you are there. I've often been in a situation where a one-man band business comes to me and starts being so humble, quietly spoken and apologetic that we hardly made it past the pleasantries. Be confident in your message. It makes a huge amount of difference.

Don't - fall into the trap of speaking and not listening. A big part of selling your services is understanding your would-be client's needs. If you don't shut up for a second and start hearing what they are saying, you could miss something really important.

Don't- stick to the same pitch. There is little point preparing a great pitch for your company, seeing it go down well and then hanging on to it like grim death. No, as your company grows and evolves, so should your account of what you can do. All the time. Once you have trained your brain to do this, it should become a natural thing for you to do. Treat it as a sixth sense tapping into the mind of the others. Most importantly, make sure you can deliver the end result too. That way, there is no fibbing either. Exaggeration is really bad and annoying and you always get caught out down the line.

Working on your perfect pitch will mean you will always put your best foot forward, whatever the circumstance, and will work every meeting to your best advantage. Understand the personality that you are pitching to and find some middle ground which will help you both work together in the future. After all, there is little point busting a gut to get in front of someone and then fluffing it when you get there.

There is Perception and then there is the truth, Reality

Scribble your stuff here

Week 8

Mentoring Matters

When you start out, the old principle of learning through the school of hard knocks is always an option, providing you have an endless supply of energy and determination, a bottomless wallet to finance your mistakes and lots of time on your side.

While you are struggling through, why not take the time to ask yourself whether you really need to carry on making a bunch of silly mistakes, or whether listening to someone else who has already made them and come out the other side may be a better option.

Finding a mentor can be the answer. I've mentored many businesses over the years, largely for free, sometimes for a fee, and have seen companies transform as a result. If an entrepreneur emails me, or contacts me via social networks, (twitter.com/lyndonx or uk.linkedin.com/in/lyndonwood) I am usually only too willing to share my expertise. I am always happy to give any business the time of day. I know that simple one-to-one interaction with an experienced hand can make seemingly insurmountable problems disappear and drastically save on all the wasted time and energy that goes with losing money and making mistakes.

Many times, if it is a small project, I will offer my advice for free. If it is part of a longer term reorganisation that is required, I will charge a nominal fee for a series of days working within the business.

One of my most notable successes as a mentor was with a medical business. The business was basically a private GP service, but while the doctors who ran it were undoubtedly good at diagnosing and curing illnesses, they were well out of their depth when it came to running a company successfully.

When I came along, it was obvious that although the doctors had built up a good customer base and were in demand, they were making some very basic errors. For example, their break-even point at that time was £120,000 a month, yet they were only collecting £90,000 a month in fees. It wasn't that they were not achieving their target, indeed they had more than £800,000 owed to them, they were simply 'too busy' to keep their debt under control.

They had made the basic business error of confusing a busy order book with a successful enterprise. If they had only stopped to look, they would have realised that a business is not worth a thing unless it keeps a close eye on cash flow.

As a mentor, I helped them to understand this and to find efficient ways to keep a steady flow of cash coming in. I also helped them with their marketing and suggested ways to switch to a smaller concentration of higher paying customers, rather than relying on numerous, time-consuming, yet low-paying patients. All of this is fairly basic. Well to me it is….

I have helped many other businesses in different ways too. All entrepreneurs could benefit from mentoring at one time or another. A knowledgeable and willing advisor offers a plethora of advantages because:

- A mentor is an outside individual with an entirely new perspective on your business and its problems.

- You can be completely candid with them and do not have to keep anything hidden. Everything you tell them will be reflected back to you in an objective way because neither side will have anything to prove.

- An outsider will be able to offer a new view gathered from experiences completely outside your sphere of knowledge. Sometimes this new viewpoint is exactly what the doctor ordered (excuse the pun) when it comes to solving a stale or persistent problem.

Without this fresh perspective, you may never move beyond your present circumstances. Indeed, if you carry on going it alone, you may seriously impair your ability to lead others beyond their existing limitations.

Hopefully, the obvious retort to this advice is; great, where do I get one?

This is, of course, the nub of the issue.

At the time of writing this book, the government has just launched its own mentoring scheme. The idea behind the new initiative is to fill the gap created by the closure of its Business Link advice centres, which shut up shop in Autumn 2011. Politicians have made lofty comments about wanting 35,000 mentors in place within a year.

That would all be terrific were it not for the fact that the core of the national mentoring scheme is to be staffed by current and former bank managers. I almost laughed when I saw this. What on earth does a bank manager know about being a business mentor? They might know about mortgages and current accounts, but I have never yet met a bank manager who can tell me anything useful about my business.

If you want to get something valuable out of a mentoring relationship, you need someone who has been there, seen it and done it. In other words: if you want to be great at riding a bike, then ride a bike, don't row a boat. You don't want someone who has just talked about it. Just because you've put someone on a course to show them how to be a business mentor doesn't mean that they'll have anything to add.

In my opinion (as someone who has seen it and done it) you will be a lot better off being a bit choosy in identifying your mentor.

The two most obvious avenues you might try are to:

- Identify a business/business leader who you admire and approach them. As I said, I am more than happy to pass on the benefit of my experience and I know that many of my entrepreneurial colleagues are just the same.

- Talk to friends, family, old colleagues, trade associations and business contacts, to see if they know anyone with relevant experience and it does not have to be in the industry you are in. Business is business.

Remember too, you don't need to confine yourself to one expert in a particular field. In fact, you would be better off with a whole series of mentors who will be able to advise on a host of different areas. Similarly, different mentors will be applicable at different times of your business development.

The key to a good mentor/protégé relationship is listening to the good advice you get. There is nothing more galling for a mentor than when they pass on the benefit of their hard-won experience and agree actions only for the recipient to completely ignore it. It's happened to me on a few occasions and it drives me mad. It also ensures that my mentoring relationship is usually cut pretty short. The perfect protégé knows the value of listening, not talking. Embrace negative feedback because it is the best way to learn.

The best mentoring relationships work in both directions. I certainly learned many new ideas from my doctor friends as indeed I have benefited from the other companies I have worked with. Everyone can benefit.

Strive for Perfection in your business

Scribble your stuff here

Week 9

When to ignore advice

In 1995, when I was just a little over five years into running my business, my accountant advised me that I should register as a limited company.

"It will be tax beneficial," he said.

Although I have always been pretty financially savvy, back then I simply took my accountant at his word and did not look too deeply into it. It did not occur to me to question the advice from this apparent expert. I told him to go ahead, signed the paperwork and became the proud CEO and managing director of a limited company.

For a while.

Three months later, my accountant went bust! He was only a small, one-man band business and clearly had not been up to much. I then had to cast around to find a replacement accountant, though this time I took a little more care with my choice, after being let down by one supposed expert. Then, the bombshell hit.

After handing over all my financial affairs to the new firm I had chosen, my accountant asked if we could have a meeting.

"Why did you become a limited company?" he asked, looking perplexed. "There is no advantage to you whatsoever at this stage. In fact, the only business that will benefit is your auditor."

He went through the reasoning in detail and I could see he was right, so I began the process to revert to my original status. I'd like to say that was the end of it. It wasn't. Although things were pretty straightforward with Companies House and I didn't even have to file accounts because I had been limited so briefly, a major publication in the insurance industry picked up the story that my company had stopped trading as a limited company. They put two and two together and made five, splashing with the headline that my business had gone into voluntary liquidation.

Almost 100 per cent of my business dried up overnight because the insurance brokers I worked with read the magazine and assumed I had ceased trading altogether. It was a complete mess, which took months to unravel; my first five hard years of business lost, gone. All because I had chosen to blindly follow the advice of an 'expert'. I couldn't even sue anyone because I didn't have the money to pay lawyers.

I did, of course, eventually recover, but the experience taught me a valuable lesson. Always, always question the advice given to you - even if the person giving it is an expert in the field. Although it is great to use consultants now and again (see Week 26: Real Approach to Business), that doesn't mean you no longer need to keep your wits about you. It is not a way of passing the buck.

Everyone in business is always bombarded with advice and a lot of it can be very useful. The trouble is, as I have found, a lot can be pretty destructive too. I have, over the years, compiled a mental list of the most common (and most useless) pieces of advice which I have been given. I have included them here, and would say that if you hear any of the following phrases, take them with a large pinch of salt.

That'll never work.
This statement has been trotted out to entrepreneurs around the globe for centuries. The President of the Michigan Savings Bank advised Henry Ford's lawyer that "the automobile is only a novelty, a fad" and would never replace horses. Ken Olsen, the founder of Digital Equipment Corp, said in 1977 that no one would ever want a computer in their home. JK Rowling was rejected by a publisher because children are not "interested in witches and wizards anymore". Enough said. "That'll never work" is a very bad piece of advice and should always be ignored.

You need money to make money.

No you don't. The best entrepreneurs make money out of their own ingenuity and wit. I started with less than nothing and built a successful business. If you want to do something badly enough, you'll make it happen.

Don't leave the day job until your start-up has revenue.

Similar to above, this well meaning advice is followed by so many poor souls who do their nine to five and then work into the wee hours of the night on their business. This is rubbish. If you are going to start a business - start it. Otherwise you are just not taking it seriously and simply playing around.

It works for me.

It is great to hear the advice of others who have been there and done it (and I know that is what I am doing in this diary, before you say anything). Just remember though to make sure that it is the right advice for you. Every business is different, our goals are different and our clients are different. Before rushing headlong to follow an expert, make sure it works for you too.

Cut your prices to increase your customer base.

Well meaning advisors say if you slash your prices in half, you could double your client base. Great - so you will be working twice as hard for the same money? That just doesn't make sense. Set your prices according to the value you provide.

Grab every customer you can.

That sounds great for some businesses, but it doesn't work for everyone. If you only have the capacity to look after X number of clients, shouldn't you go for the reliable/big payers first? There is no point scrabbling around to keep the numbers up.

Never give up.
Dogged determination is great. Flogging a dead horse is not. If there is something wrong in your business, don't keep slogging away in the belief that if you work hard, you will get your due rewards. You won't. You are just gonna get knackered and probably go out of business. Instead, stop, take a breather and work out what is going wrong. Then, work hard at putting it right.

You are growing too quickly.
There is no such thing. If you are growing fast and have everything under control, such as your infrastructure and profit margins, what right has anyone got to tell you that? I sacked my first business bank when they said that to me.

Remember - everyone has an opinion, but not all of those opinions are always based on facts and sometimes those opinions are fuelled by self-interest. Plus, just because someone appears to be highly knowledgeable, you should always be the best judge of what works best for you.

I always listen to rational expert advice, but I also always take the lead in dictating which direction my business goes in. Make a point of challenging the status quo and be wary of the supposed 'rules' which others vaguely refer to when they are trying to tell you something can't be done.

Just Do It

Scribble your stuff here

Week 10

Theory is naff - Trust your instincts

Watching TV the other day, I came across a Canadian version of the UK *Dragons' Den* show. In this programme, there was the usual panel of successful multi-millionaire business people, who were vying to invest their hard-earned cash in the entrepreneurs of tomorrow.

This particular episode featured a bunch of enterprising students, who sufficiently impressed the panel to secure investment for their new business idea. Then, in a slight variation of the format of the UK show, the programme followed the students through the early stages of development following the cash injection.

The programme tracked the youngsters to a boardroom setting where they were talking strategy with their new Dragon investors. For some reason, their university tutor was in on the meeting. All of a sudden, as the plans were thrashed out on a flip chart, the tutor hopped up to his feet and started getting very agitated.

"Do you have an MBA, or business degree?" he demanded from the (slightly bemused) panel of Dragons with a combined wealth of in excess of $850 million.

The subtext was clear. If the Dragons did not have a string of qualifications behind them and letters after their names declaring them to be experts in leveraged finance, or business finance, or advanced negotiations, they were clearly not qualified to be leading these students forward.

My jaw nearly dropped to the floor. Collectively these investors were worth hundreds of millions of dollars, thanks to their successful business ventures. The fact that they had or hadn't (and as it turned out most of them hadn't) gone to university was totally irrelevant. They had good, solid experience of the real world and had excelled in it to boot.

This incident really resonated with me. As I have said before, I left school at 14-years-old with no qualifications to my name, yet have gone on to build up businesses worth millions of pounds. Plus, I have provided employment to hundreds of people over the years too, as well as provided life changing career opportunities for them.

At school, I hated reading what so-called experts felt I should be looking at. I also really resented the fact that I was discouraged from learning about the stuff I was interested in. I am not alone. There are many billionaires who resolutely play by their own rules and only focus on what they are interested in, and guess what? They didn't do so well at school either. They just had no interest in theory and wanted to go out into the real world to try things out.

At the other end of the scale are those who hide behind business theory when they have little or no practical experience in the workplace. These people infuriate me. They use it to mask a lack of understanding of what business is really about, or worse still to stall on dealing with any real issues.

I see this most when dealing with outside consultants and, to be honest, when I become aware of it, I always become very wary in my dealings with that person or company. I do also come across it a lot with job applicants too.

I often say to them, I am not interested in MBAs and degrees. Theory is just theory and the real world is very different. I'm more interested in hearing about their experience and their success in dealing with real life issues. The most successful fortune hunters get out there and get things done. They learn by experimenting, trying new things and occasionally falling flat on their face.

Preferring the experience approach may mean you have to take some risks or take some leaps of faith. You may even screw up now and again. That's fine. I always value people with a few scars, because they steered away from the safer theory route, endured the challenges and overcame them.

I feel very strongly that if you spend all your time learning, you'll be able to talk a good game but you won't actually get anywhere.

Why is experience so important? Well, think about it this way; if you read an article, or guidebook, about somewhere you have never been, you won't ever get as familiar with it as if you had been there yourself. It is much easier to remember experiences over theory.

"Ah," you may say, "this is a book about how to make your fortune as an entrepreneur and that's theory, isn't it?" And so it is. But, this question raises a very important point: not all theory is bad.

Bear with me - I am not about to contradict myself.

Throughout my business career, I have constantly reached for books, or turned to the internet to find out things I don't know. If I ever think that I have a gap in my knowledge, then I go and find out what others have done in similar situations. Then, I go out and put the theory into practice, refining it along the way and adjusting it according to my own personal needs. I don't stick rigidly to the rules, or doggedly follow any step-by-step formulas, but use my research as a starting point.

So, yes, I do use theory all the time. The point to remember is: you need learning and experience to drive you forward, but it is the experience that really makes you go places.

This book is simply a guide that sets down my own personal real life experiences and gives advice as to how it might work for you. I would, however, be the first to say that you won't become a successful entrepreneur by just reading books (or by taking courses for that matter). You've got to get off your butt and try things for yourself.

If you take the experience approach, it is essential to take the time to review the lessons you learn along the way too. After finding a way to tackle problems or move something forward, reflect on what you did to make it happen. What have you learned from it? How could you use that knowledge next time? If you carry on battling forward, but never take the time to absorb your knowledge, you'll be no better off than if you had sat in a classroom taking in nothing. There is such a thing as trying too hard as well.

Plus, if you take time to reflect, you'll have a good stock of practical examples to impart, should some smart alec ever start questioning your suitability to run a business. That could stop you from saying something you shouldn't!

So, my advice is, don't hold back and get sucked in to do a business degree or MBA before starting your quest for a fortune. It's just an excuse and a delaying tactic. Get in there and get on with it. Find out what you need to know along the way. Don't ever let anyone tell you they know better because they have letters after their name. They don't.

Never settle for versions of your vision

Scribble your stuff here

Week 11

Naff Business Set-ups - Take risks but learn from your mistakes!

If you are reading this diary, or know anything about my insurance group, you may well be thinking I am a pretty successful guy. You'd be right. I have done well and I live an extremely comfortable life. What you may not have guessed though is that, over the years, I have lost £175,000 on failed business ventures. No, that is not a typo, I really have lost that much. I could well even lose the same amount again.

Perhaps though, before I pave the way for future cock-ups, I had better fess up to my failures so far.

The first of my corporate fatalities was a publishing business and I will outline that sorry tale in more detail in Week 13. For now, I will tell you that in five months I managed to shed £35,000 and ended up laying off my own father and stepmother to get out of the mess. That was obviously not an ideal scenario.

The second screw-up was an internet firm I started called ceowner.com. This website offered fellow company owners forums on a range of business subjects. Though I say so myself, it was an awesome site, offering all sorts of stuff like instant messaging, forums, photo and document libraries, plus it could act as a pure intranet as well. Information could be either public or private at the click of a mouse.

Then, after investing £110,000 on the software and source code, I had to pull the plug on ceowner.com. Why? After 18 months of development (including employing someone to run the site), I realised that social networks like this need a lot more than a great piece of back-end kit if they stand any chance of being able to hold their own in the crowded world wide web. I simply did not have the resources, finance, time or enthusiasm to take ceowner.com where it needed to go so I cut it loose. The upside is I still own all the IP.

The third big failure was with an online accessories retailer for men called Axsori.com. Again, I invested in software and source code to build up a sophisticated retail web operation that enabled me to manage stock, prices, images, offers, deals and orders. I also bought a big stock of items such as cufflinks, ties, belts, shorts, sunglasses and watches that I intended to sell on Axsori.com.

After an investment of £30,000, I could see Axsori.com was not going to work as I had hoped. There was a range of reasons. I had (yet again) broken my rule of not working with family members and had put my nephew in charge of the fledgling venture. However, as I had other businesses to attend to, I underestimated the help and guidance that he needed. Unfortunately, my nephew did not have the background to be able to rise to the challenge either. It was not his fault; he was just 20 years of age and has since gone on to establish his very own bespoke tailoring business. The timing was just wrong.

Another major deciding factor was my experience with the suppliers we approached. To be honest, I found them rather ignorant and obstructive, which was crazy to me because we could have all benefited if the company had taken off. I guess it takes all sorts, but these suppliers clearly did not have an entrepreneurial bone between them.

So, on to the £175,000 of my hard-earned fortune that I could yet still lose on more failed ventures. Am I crazy? No. In fact, I welcome these failures because I have learned so much from them and will do so again.

Failures are an opportunity for fortune hunters. In fact, failure is the greatest teacher you will ever know. If you don't fail, you are just not trying hard enough.

Think about it. What makes a successful business owner? What puts them streets ahead? What makes them millions when others are scrabbling around for pennies?

Risk

If you think big, you will get the big rewards. You will also fall on your arse a few times too. But, as long as you get it right more times than you get it wrong, then you are quids in.

The trouble with society today (and I never thought I would reach an age where I would say this, let alone believe it) is that we are too success orientated. Everyone celebrates the triumphs and breakthroughs and hides away the bad bits. Over time, businesses get increasingly risk-adverse because they can't bear the shame of not making the grade. Yet, companies need to take risks in order the foster the innovation and creativity which lead to the big steps forward.

Another element of this success orientated culture is that it breeds complacency. It's the old "if it ain't broke, don't fix it" syndrome. Companies which started with all sorts of verve, energy and great ideas, start coasting along. What happens next is they gradually lose the momentum all together and grind to a halt.

Imagine though, if you were constantly striving to move forward, taking a few risks and chalking up a few failures on the way. Every time something goes wrong, you will examine it in minute detail. Why didn't it work? Did I miss something? This prompt examination of your errors will pervade every part of your business. It means that everything will be under constant scrutiny and will never, ever be allowed to coast.

For example, one of the reasons behind at least some of my failures was I lost interest. This showed me how important it is to keep passion in a business, because once that goes, it is really hard to pull back. Once I realised this, it forced me to re-examine, and renew, my feelings about my core businesses.

When things go wrong, it makes you broaden your thinking. You won't just think about why that particular part of your business, or new division, or new product, turned out to be such a dud. You will be forced into identifying all the elements that went into that failure. It might be that you'll spot those same elements in your existing, successful, operations. Then, you'll start asking yourself whether the fact that the other bits of your empire are OK is sheer good luck, or whether there is the potential for a similar problem in something you had previously thought was fine. Once you start thinking like this, you will be able to make all the necessary adjustments before those same things start to erode your business elsewhere.

I am not saying that it won't be painful to lose tens of thousands of pounds. It is and always will be. The point to remember is; these setbacks, however personally and professionally damaging, will teach you more than any business textbook or mentor ever could. Learning from the school of hard knocks is never easy, but it is just that; learning. The worst thing you could ever do is start believing in your own infallibility. Stay focused, keep trying things and you will grow stronger through every twist and turn. Apart from anything else, those howlers will make great stories to tell the grandkids one day, or maybe you could put them into your very own book.

Appreciate employees have desires too

Scribble your stuff here

_____

_____

_____

_____

_____

_____

_____

_____

_____

_____

_____

Week 12

Taking your business to the next stage

For most people, starting their business is the most important step. Maybe they had to give up a steady job, or risk some serious money on their dream, or plough on determinedly against the clamour of cautionary advice from the naysayers.

If they've hit it right, got a good idea and are prepared to put the hours in, the chances are they'll be feeling a bit better about it all. If they are really fortunate, they may even have more orders than they know how to cope with. They may even be constantly firefighting and finding it isn't such a lot of fun anymore, increased income or no increased income. At this point, it may dawn on them that they face a far bigger challenge than before.

If this is the position you are in, the question you need to ask yourself is; how do I expand my business to take it to the next, higher, level? If you are a true fortune hunter, it is a matter you need to address and fast, before you get to the stage where you are losing business because you don't have the scale or processes to cope with it.

Funnily enough, this is often the sticking point that is the undoing of many ambitious small businesses.

Stepping up from a small business to a medium, or even large, one is a quandary that all businesses will face at some point. Get it wrong and your expansion plans can easily go awry and you could even end up jeopardising everything you have worked so hard to build. Timing is, of course, an all-important factor too. If you react too slowly, your business may stagnate. Move too fast and you run the risk of making yourself vulnerable in a competitive marketplace.

To make the process easier, and help you to plan your growth strategy, I have compiled a list of questions that you may like to consider before you make any big moves. Take some time to answer them all honestly and fully before you make any big commitments:

1.   **Understand your profit centres.**
      Where do you make your most profit and your least?
      Can you (easily) obtain more of the product to sell or the service you offer?

2.   **Look at the trends of your customers.**
      Is the market growing or shrinking? For your business to flourish, there must be sufficient demand.
      Are there any emerging trends or technologies which might indicate a decline or increase in the sector?

3.   **Is the market big enough for your product or service?**
      Clearly, for your business to flourish, there needs to be enough demand for the products or services you offer.

4.   **Put numbers on everything.**
      How much do you want to realistically make?
      By when?
      How many extra staff will it take?
      How much extra stock will you need, if any?
      Will you need to extend your premises, or even move to a completely new building?

5. **How much will it all cost, and where will you obtain the funding?**
Being careful not to overstretch your finances and with one eye on what you will need to keep pace with the increase in volume, will you get money from any of the following sources: Banks (hard to do in the current climate)?
Government loan?
Own money?
Private investor?
(Remember to consider what will happen if demand for your products or service is seasonal or irregular. Will your extra cash get you through the peaks and troughs which will occur over a period of time?)

6. **How will you market your product or service to grow?**
Do you have a marketing plan (keep it simple)?
Have you thought about all the distribution channels (online, offline, partners)?
Is your website up-to-date (it's the first place people look)?

The next, most crucial, stage is to put your plan down in writing onto a PC, Mac or even iPad. Does it make good reading? Or are there just too many unknowns? If there are, go back to the beginning of this list and work on putting some realistic numbers to your plan. This will form the basis of your measurement of success.

Next, share your plans with your team. What do they think? They may well have some feedback that you have not considered, simply because they see a different side to the business on a day-to-day basis. Plus, give some thought to the fact that your relationship with your close-knit team may well change as you scale up and you may have to change your usual hands-on, management style. Apart from anything else, you need to find a way to make your existing team continue to feel valued and listened to, particularly during a period of change.

Finally, when you are pretty sure you have a good business plan - make it happen. Many people talk a good game. If you want to succeed, you cannot be one of them. So, press the button and make it fly. Give the expanded venture the resources it needs to take it to the next stage.

It may be that, as you continue down the line, you find that things do not turn out exactly as you predicted. That's fine. In fact, it probably will happen. Just adapt your plan, go back to basics, put some numbers on it and plough on. Similarly, keep a constant eye on results. If things are not working out as you expected, even if they are working a whole lot better than you ever imagined, find out why. If you need to, adjust, do so and move forward. I look at results of my sales force daily and in some areas three times a day. That way you can very quickly act on anything good or bad. You should never leave it to the end of the month.

Scaling up is not just about doing more of what you currently do now. Problems that you never have even realised you had in a smaller business will be amplified significantly when you grow to any scale. The businesses that survive this metamorphosis are the ones that plan ahead, identify any barriers and constantly monitor the change.

Your motivations for growing your business will most likely be as personal as why you started it in the first place. The important thing is that you are prepared and able to manage the growth.

Summary

There are no certainties when starting a business, and new companies fail all the time. You can, however, vastly increase your odds of success by preparing well, listening to the right advice and not ignoring your instincts.

The most important lesson in this section is that you need to get off your butt, stop thinking about your dream and actually do something about it to make it fly. A new business idea is only ever an idea until you make it happen.

After that, things will start to fall into place.

You will make some mistakes along the way and that is fine. In fact, you should be worried if you don't because that means you are not pushing yourself hard enough. The best thing is you are now on your way. Doesn't that feel good?

SUMMER

So, you've started your business and it looks pretty good.

Now is the time to get it really soaring to make the fortune you deserve. Here's how to boost your armoury with everything from a talented and dedicated workforce, to some great marketing and PR.

Respect your employees and help them learn

Scribble your stuff here

Week 13

Don't keep things in the family - ever!
(And leave friends out of it too)

In my long list of entrepreneurial ventures, I once flirted for a brief while with becoming a publishing giant. However, my experience of setting up a magazine was an abject failure. My mistake? I ignored all the warnings about being cautious when employing friends or family. In fact, I went one step further into the mire and took on both!

Let me relate this painful tale in more detail. It all began with a mate who I had got to know at my local fitness club. He was a charming guy and a graphic designer by trade, making about £50,000 a year doing odd design jobs, which included running a magazine for the gym where we trained.

Early on in the recession, it quickly became clear that my pal was having a really tough time and was on the verge of going out of business. On the spur of the moment, I decided to take over the magazine and let him run it. I convinced myself that I quite fancied being a publisher and thought my mate was the ideal person to run my new business. That was mistake number one.

I then compounded the error by inviting my father and stepmother in to help run the magazine and sell advertising space. They too had fallen on hard times and I thought it might help them back on their feet. This was mistake number two.

In a very short space of time, I could see that this magazine was not making enough money to cover its costs. In fact, it wasn't even close to being a commercial venture.

So, I took a trip to the magazine's office to take a look at the business to see if I could help in some way. The place was like the Mary Celeste. No one was there to answer the phone, which clearly presented a bit of a problem if people wanted to call and spend their money on advertising or a subscription.

When I finally gathered the trio together, I asked them a few pertinent questions such as; where were they, and why weren't they able to sell more space?

It turned out that it had not even occurred to them that it might be a problem that there was no one around to take orders while they were out 'selling'. Equally worrying was the fact that they apparently had no idea how much space they needed to sell in order to break-even.

I gave them a chance and talked them through the reverse planning of their costs. I showed them that the fixed cost of the magazine was £x and if they charged £x for 10 different ads to fill it, they would meet their costs. They all nodded gravely and then went back to business as usual! Or no business, as it turned out.

By this time, I had had enough and decided to put a stop to it. I closed the business down. Needless to say, all three were now out of work (which I may add I hated to see, but it was costing me, not them). The whole experience was a disaster and obviously soured my relationship with everyone concerned.

I'd like to say that this was the one and only time that I have broken my cardinal rule of not employing friends and family. It isn't. I am ashamed to admit that I have been a bit of a soft touch over the years. Being like this has cost me dear. I reckon I have wasted the best part of £100,000 over the last few years giving close friends and family a helping hand.

Aside from the financial cost, there have been other repercussions too. I have discovered that employing friends and family can:

- *Cause resentment among existing employees.* Even if you are not favouring your kith and kin, other people in your firm always imagine that you are paying them better, or giving them priority in decisions over matters, such as annual leave or promotions.

- *Disrupt your personal relationships with those close to you.* As I showed above, when you have to make tough decisions at times like this, it can have a serious knock-on affect on your home life. (My brother-in-law didn't speak to my wife or me for 10 years following another misguided family and friends' venture) Plus, you often don't just fall out with them; the conflict can spread to other family and friends.

- *Create a new and unwelcome culture in your business.* Family and friends are more likely to take advantage in a way they would never do with a regular job. They may not adhere to business hours; they may insist on a longer holiday allowance and might even do things like bringing in their children or pets to work with them. All of this will add to the atmosphere of distrust and disrespect.

- *Change the way you deal with potentially high conflict situations.* You are far more likely to delay making crucial decisions if they are likely to cause conflict with those close to you. This failure to clear the air and do what needs to be done creates unwanted stress and a build-up of frustration.

- *Challenge your authority.* As the company founder, you should always have the final say in any decisions; however friends and family are far more likely to question you, even in public. Plus, knowing you well, they are more likely to attack you on a personal level if they feel provoked to make a point.

Clearly, despite proclaiming not to employ friends and family, I have not followed my own advice. I have, as I have already admitted, even repeated my own error time and again. So, for your sake as well as mine, here are a few rules to mitigate some of the damage if you do find yourself in a position of employing someone close to you.

- *Choose wisely.* Assess the person's skills in the same detached manner that you would use for any other candidate. What are their abilities, strengths and weaknesses? If the friend or family has a limited skill set, they are only ever likely to apply that skill, and will neglect all the other work and you will be setting them up to fail before they start.

- *Set boundaries.* Create and enforce a policy that you never discuss work on personal time and never talk about personal issues in the office.

- *Put it in writing.* Draw up a detailed document which covers your business agreement before loved ones join you. It is easier to avoid conflict and misunderstandings if everyone knows up-front what they are expected to achieve. This should also be your normal way of employing anyone anyway.

- Finally, there is one golden rule. And this one, I have at least managed to adhere to. That rule is: *never hire family or friends unless you are prepared to fire them.*

However, if you can be more strong-minded on this one than I have been (and are serious about making your fortune), leave the family and friends at home. It would be better for all concerned to find some other way to help them.

Knowledge is not just power, it is a greater way to build your business

Scribble your stuff here

Week 14

Good Drivers…brrrrrooommm - How to cope with employees

Once your business gets to any size, you'll need to take on staff. Sadly, I have to tell you that when dealing with employees, it can often feel like you are walking through a bloody minefield. One day, you will walk in and ask if everything is OK and it will be all smiles. The next day, you'll ask the same question and someone will rush off in tears while their colleagues shake their heads in collective despair.

In my experience as a fortune hunter, learning how to deal with and motivate my staff has always been far, far, more troublesome and complex than actually working out how to sell more product or scale up my firm.

I'll make no bones about it - sometimes it has been a complete nightmare.

Obviously you can't ignore the vexed question of keeping staff happy to get on with what you need to do alone. It stands to reason that you'll never be able to do anything of scale without a bunch of people around you. Yet, once you start building up any number of staff, if you don't get it right, the effects of low employee motivation on a young or growing business can be devastating. The problems range from complacency, to declining morale, to widespread lethargy. If these issues are allowed to fester, they'll inevitably lead to reduced productivity, earnings and competitiveness.

Yet oddly, this is a side to entrepreneurialism that rarely gets talked about. Most business books or articles, which talk up the rags to riches tale of one hugely successful business or another, rarely mention the mountains that need to be climbed back at the office.

You need to start by understanding that, just because you live and breathe your business doesn't mean your staff will do the same. In fact, it is a complete rarity to find any employees with even a tenth of the energy, commitment and creativity of the average entrepreneur (and, yes, I know there is no such thing as 'an average' entrepreneur!). Plus, since an employee's every waking moment is not consumed by plotting and planning how to grow the business more quickly, they are much more prone to get distracted by petty domestic disputes or meaningless distractions at work.

Frustrating? You don't know the half of it.

The answer, as I have learned through painful trial and error, is in two parts.

The first is to surround yourself with 'real' people. These are the people who do actually care about being part of your business (i.e. it is not just a job to them). They want to do right by the business, have great work ethics and, by and large, they want to do right by you. (For clues about spotting these real people at the interview stage, see 'Week 15: Ten Year Club - Finding (and keeping) the best staff')

The next part is to find out what motivates, or drives them.

"Ah," you may be thinking, "you mean money." Yes, financial incentives will help, but they are not the be all and end all. In fact, money is always a pretty poor driver in my experience and only works for short periods of time. As a matter of course, I have always given my employees an inflation linked annual pay rise, which is pretty generous by today's standards. But it is still not enough for some people. Expectations often exceed results and the motivational effect is always pretty short-lived. Most people will soon forget about the annual raise. Throwing money at the problem is not the answer.

Linking financial incentives to performance can help. You could, for example, reward employees for generating cost savings, or process improving ideas to boost productivity or reduce absenteeism. But, this can divide and demotivate some who think others are being recognised, while their efforts are being ignored. You'll never please everyone this way.

To be effective, the monetary incentives have to be linked with other good drivers, such as:

- *Learning*. Employees who are given the tools and opportunities to accomplish more will willingly take on more challenges. If you commit to helping your staff to learn more and enhance their skills, it will bolster their self-confidence and their attitude towards the company. (See Week 16: Knowledge partners)

- *Creativity and innovation*. Employees will often not express their creative ideas to management for fear of ridicule. This culture could have become ingrained without you even realising it, perhaps because you have a bad manager of a particular department, or another member of staff is regularly taking the mickey out of his or her colleagues. If you think this is happening, find out where and deal with it. Give your staff the power to be creative and open with their ideas.

- *Quality of life*. Many workers find it increasingly hard to meet the demands of life beyond work. If two adults in a household are working, childcare can be a real juggle. If you can find a way around it and introduce flexible working arrangements, you will keep motivated and happy employees forever. Flexitime and job-sharing will focus overwhelmed employees away from the demands of their private lives and on to the job in hand.

- *Stretch and challenge*. Contrary to popular belief, people do like to work. There is nothing more demotivating than having time on your hands. Make sure employees are stretched and have plenty to keep them busy.

- *Responsibility.* Give your employees more decision-making responsibility to increase their control over the tasks for which they are responsible. Everyone likes to feel ownership over what they do and if you give them this power, it will decrease their frustration over being held accountable for things over which they feel they have no control.

- *Say "thank you".* Yes, those two little words can make a real difference. They are simple to say and stretching it to buying the team an occasional drink to celebrate their success will result to improved productivity, better morale and a happier team.

Believe it or not, a small or medium sized business can actually be the ideal atmosphere for driving the ambitions of the right people because they'll be able to see the results of their contributions in a much more immediate way than in large firms.

The right people will thrive in businesses which create positive working environments and that in turn will increase your enjoyment of running the business. The key is finding them and then creating the drivers to move you all forward together at a good rapid pace.

Cash is King and Queen

Scribble your stuff here

_____

_____

_____

_____

_____

_____

_____

_____

_____

_____

_____

_____

_____

Week 15

Ten Year Club - Finding (and keeping) the best staff

Like most business leaders, I've made mistakes in recruitment. The worst ones are usually when I don't listen to my instincts and allow myself to be influenced by other people.

I should have read the signs when I asked a would-be marketing director to do a 20 minute presentation to the board for his second interview and he ended up rambling on for nearly an hour. While all my instincts screamed "Don't recruit this man", I somehow got diverted by the fact that he said all the right things (albeit really slowly) and asked the right questions. We took him on and, sure enough, he was a complete nightmare. Funnily enough, it was not his lack of succinctness that was the problem. It was that he was completely negative about anyone else's ideas, including mine. His catchphrase was, "No, that won't work". He didn't have what it took to be a part of a fast-moving, ambitious entrepreneurial set-up and I should have known that from the start. After six months and countless chances, I had to let him go.

Ignoring your gut feelings aside, it is not easy to find good people, particularly if you are a small or medium sized company. All the so-called experts advise you to get the best people you can because having the right people is so crucial. That's great and I agree wholeheartedly in principle. The trouble is, when you are starting out, most of the best people wouldn't touch you with a bargepole. Why would they, when they can easily get well-paid and secure jobs at bigger firms? Who would risk their income on a firm with less than 10 people and an uncertain future?

It is far better to start off with the mindset that you will get the best people you can get. If you are careful with your recruitment (and don't get side-tracked by showy one hour long presentations), you will find people who will do the job and hopefully grow with you emotionally and intellectually.

The first important lesson in finding these gems is not to get carried away by an applicant's inflated view of their own worth. In recent years, as the economy becomes increasingly squeezed, I am constantly being approached by people who think they are worth a lot more money than they are. These are usually folks who have recently been made redundant from some high-flying job. They may have been at that job for 20 years and over that time will have seen a steady rise in their salary through generous annual increments. By the time they leave, they will be on a respectable £80,000 a year and will be hell-bent on a mission to realise that salary in their new job. The trouble is, they are not worth it. In fact, the reason they were probably laid off is because it was glaringly obvious that they were being paid too much.

Sometimes it is hard to see through all this crap when you are looking for good senior people. I manage it by constantly reminding myself that I know my business inside out and upside down. I know what good people are worth and I'm not prepared to overpay, impressive CV or no impressive CV.

I always make sure I sit in on key interviews too, because I don't believe in delegating such an important task to my staff. By doing this, I have learned the odd trick along the way - notwithstanding the odd cock-up.

My approach is to keep things quite informal and friendly because if you act in this way, candidates will relax and become informal too. When people start to relax, you see much more of their true character. That is when they'll start inadvertently letting things out of the bag.

So, for instance, I may ask about their notice period.

A relaxed interviewee, sensing he or she is on the home straight, may say something like: "Oh, don't worry. I won't need to give much notice. I'll just leave anyway, so I can start as soon as you like."

They may see that as a positive. I don't. I am just thinking; they'd do that to me one day and leave me in the lurch for a better offer. If anyone says something like that, forget it.

The other thing that is guaranteed to see me propelling a candidate out of the door quicker than you can say, "You are a completely hopeless applicant" is people who make no effort whatsoever to find out about my company. I always make a point of asking people, "What do you know about the Moorhouse Group?" I am amazed that eight out of 10 people will only be able to say, "It is an insurance company."

How difficult is it to Google Moorhouse Group and read our website? If you honestly wanted a job paying £15,000 plus a year, never mind £30,000 plus, don't you think it is a matter of common courtesy to find out who you are talking to? Why on earth should I waste an hour of my time talking to someone this lazy and ill-informed?

My biggest pet hate is people who come to me with a big business mentality. They'll ask questions like, "What's the budget of this department?" I always reply, "There isn't one, because I expect you to generate your own income." Any fool can spend money if there is a pot of cash. I want to see entrepreneurial thinkers, who are working out how to move things forward with the smallest possible outlay, preferably nothing. Apart from anything else, I want them to blend in with my culture. I need people who are free-thinkers, target driven and willing to roll up their sleeves to help out elsewhere when needed. They have to be able to chip in because there is not an army to take up the slack if they fancy a quiet life.

Reading this, you may think that with my tough entry requirements, I don't manage to get many people on board. I do and I have. What's more, when I get someone that meets my high standards, I do everything I can to keep hold of them.

To me, a loyal, long term member of staff is worth a handful of new joiners. I have people who have stayed with me through thick and thin, and who have been with my company for 10 years or more. I have celebrated this by creating the Ten Year Club and never fail to point them out to anyone I show around the business. Like it or not, even in the current climate, it is never easy to retain good staff. There is a secret to getting employees into the Ten Year Club and it is not about money. It is about creating good advocates. Yes, the beauty about the Ten Year Club is it is self-sustaining. The more people you employ who say good things about the company, the more others will want to stay.

Finding and keeping good people is not rocket science. Listen to your instincts, keep your bullshit radar firmly switched on and ask the right questions. You won't go far wrong.

Be a Dealmaker

Scribble your stuff here

Week 16

Knowledge partners - how to help staff to reach their full potential

Every one of us, from the chief executive of a blue chip company, to a lowly office worker, has great knowledge. It is how you use that expertise that makes all the difference in your life.

I've often reflected on how I have recruited fantastic people into my businesses because they have experience in what they do but then, once they get through the door, the majority seem to forget that experience and just do what is asked of them, rather than use what they know. They never seem to realise their full potential.

But, reflecting on such issues, or worse still becoming frustrated by them, is not a good position for a fortune hunter to be in. I decided to get to the root of the problem and see if there was a way that my team could be made to work better for me to support my quest for greater profits and security for everyone.

Breaking down the issue, I saw that my workforce fell into two divisions: those that knew what they were doing, but didn't really use their business acumen to the full, and the handful of shining stars who went the extra mile in everything they did, using the benefit of their previous experience and education.

None of this had anything to do with being bright. Or having a string of qualifications from top notch educational establishments. It was all to do with application. Those shining stars had application in spades and I christened them knowledge partners.

Spotting the knowledge partners

Knowledge workers are generally individuals who keep to themselves and get on with the job they are employed to do. They often take time to do other tasks that they were not specifically contracted to do too. You won't find them around the water cooler discussing last night's episode of *Coronation Street*.

Not surprisingly, knowledge workers get their work done to a higher standard, have a greater understanding of their job and the impact it has on the company as a whole.

Identifying the issues

Why is it though that the rest of my team is not like this? After all, most of my team, to a man and a woman, values knowledge and training. I have always offered extensive training facilities to all my staff. Indeed, somewhat unusually for a company that employs around 140 people, I have (at considerable expense) employed three full-time trainers offering everything from product training, to sales tips, to advice on using our systems. The team, across the board (not just the knowledge workers), has always enthusiastically embraced these opportunities.

Digging further, it became obvious that the prime motivation for taking up the training opportunities was for their personal gain. Thus, for example, one of my software developers repeatedly asked me to employ a more senior developer so she could learn more about the field from them. Her agenda was clearly that she wanted to gain this knowledge to increase her prospects on the job market. Sure enough, once she saw this opportunity was not forthcoming, she was off.

It is an understandable human instinct to want to better oneself, perhaps with a view to getting a better position, but I wanted the training to also give my team a sense of direction to help my business. I am, after all, not a charity. To be utterly selfish here, (and that is what a fortune hunter needs to be) I wanted the training I paid for to benefit my organisation and drive my profits, and not just act as a university so people can learn at my expense, and then leave with their knowledge.

Finding a solution

My challenge was to find a way to help people so they were not just motivated to become better because of personal gain, but also through a desire to feel part of the business and to contribute to its goals. The answer I found lay with my dedicated knowledge workers. They were the route to keeping the staff motivated, help them learn new concepts and to understand why these skills may impact on my firm. They could help bring everyone up to their exacting standards.

So, I put my knowledge workers in the training room to share their experience and enthusiasm with the others. Each one of my half a dozen knowledge workers was persuaded to conduct one training session a week. To guarantee their agreement to this development, I gave each one a nominal salary increase.

The benefits

The benefits of this simple reorganisation were breathtaking and worked on many levels.

- My knowledge partners became *even more* motivated because they enjoyed the opportunity to share their learning.

- Now their job was more varied, I was also able to retain these vital knowledge partners for longer too. They had no reason to look for jobs elsewhere.

- I saved a fortune on my training budget because I was able to let my team of dedicated trainers go.

- Learning with their peers helped the rest of the (non-knowledge partner) team became more focused about my company. They were more willing to learn and apply their knowledge. Plus, they too are now more likely to want to stay with the company for longer because they will feel they are getting the best training available.

- Overall, there is now a better feel to the business because I, as the business owner, know that I am building better careers for my staff.

I have always encouraged people to ask me for assistance if they have a training need and have then endeavoured to provide full facilities. However, it was not until I considered the value of my knowledge partners that I really became able to offer training that met all their needs and the needs of the business.

It can make your life so much easier - and your business so much more profitable - if you spot your knowledge partners. Even though I am paying a small salary increase to these new trainers, I have saved thousands of pounds on my training bill. By increasing the motivation and work ethic of the entire workforce, I am getting more growth and income too.

If you have knowledge partners in your company, act on it. It will make your business a better one.

Never live in the glory of it all

Scribble your stuff here

www.diaryofafortunehunter.com
Follow me on twitter@lyndonx

Week 17

Empowerment with controls - Keeping your staff on track

Do you want to know what drives me really crazy? So-called business gurus who keep banging on about staff empowerment. You know, the sort of people who say that if you give your team space and total independence, they will flourish into a world-beating force that will leave all other mere mortals trembling in their wake. It won't.

In fact, if you follow all this empowerment nonsense, you are gonna end up in a real mess. Before you know it, some numpty on your team will have gone off, completely changed some process to fit in with his or her newfound lofty view and no one will be able to access even the most simplest of data, let alone get any real work done.

That is not the only disadvantage of empowering your workforce. It can also lead to:

- *Abuse of power.* Employees can take advantage of this empowerment for their personal gain. Ask a team to develop performance standards for their section and more likely than not they will come up with ones that are easily attainable. Job done. Or job not done, as the case may be.

- *Bad relations.* You'll be opening up the way for conflict between senior staff and those lower down the ranks. Managers may have a difficult time understanding or accepting a culture of employee empowerment and wonder what they are doing there at all.

- *More training costs.* If your team is not up to the skills required for the new super-empowered dynamic, guess who is going to have to shell out for more training to get them up to speed? Apart from anything else, there is no training programme in the world that can guarantee that employee empowerment will yield positive results.

- *Insufficient knowledge.* The idea of empowerment might sound great on paper, but not all employees have the knowledge, or even the desire, to step up to the plate. The result? Poor decisions and frustration all round.

Or to put it simply:

- *Workers* should be focused on tasks and skills.

- *Managers* should manage and their focus is the mission.

- *Leaders* should lead. The leader's job is to influence people and to use the assets of his or her team.

Total empowerment does not sit easily in this business model and any moves towards empowerment should be very carefully handled.

I have seen first-hand just how badly empowerment can go wrong. A friend of mine has just seen his business go into administration because he gave too much power away to his staff. He paid his team a decent amount of money to take care of his firm and they didn't. Most crucially, the employees who were meant to be paying his bills were not paying them. By the time he realised he had a real problem, swallowed his pride and asked others for help, it was too late. The debts were too big to survive.

My friend's biggest problem was that he gave too much power away and didn't think to put any controls in place to protect himself. The result? He lost everything he was working for and was left with less than nothing.

None of this is to say that you can't, or shouldn't, give your staff their heads to make some decisions, even some critical business ones. After all, delegating some decision-making builds trust and that is a good thing. People like to be part of the solution and, as your empire grows you can't be everywhere at once. You certainly have not got time to check everything either.

The balancing trick you need to bring off is empowerment with controls.

A control mechanism can be a simple audit, or internal checks and balances to make sure things are going as you would expect. It can even be as simple as a chat over coffee or lunch. You can ask members of the team, "How is it going?" Before you know it, little things will sneak into the conversation, your alarm bells will ring and you'll be on to an issue.

Take the time to think through carefully how these checks and balances might work on a practical basis and where they may potentially fall down. I would, for example, never let my sales manager be responsible for giving me all the sales numbers. The sales manager and his or her team are expected to sell, and sell as much as they can. Their bonus structure is geared around their performance. It does not make sense to put them in charge of giving you the numbers. You should always get the sales figures done by someone who has no interest whatsoever in what the numbers look like.

Another classic control technique is to have a look around when a prominent member of your team goes on holiday. You are not being sneaky; you are merely taking the opportunity to take an overview without alarming, or demotivating, the person in question. It is a perfect time to talk to people further down the ranks in that department, because you will soon realise whether that person is doing all that you want them to do.

Lastly, I always make it very clear to everyone around me that, while I want them to feel empowered and fully endorse a great deal of autonomy, no one is ever allowed to change the systems or processes at the core of my company. Ever.

For empowerment with controls to really work, you need to be prepared to share information with everyone and give them the chance to respond. Be relaxed. Chat with people. Show that you welcome new ideas on anything at any time. Make it clear that if they've got any ideas to boost sales or make things more efficient in the back office, they are absolutely at liberty to try it and see if it flies.

None of this is about not trusting your team. It is simply about control and taking away any potential source of risk for the business.

Tap into your suppliers' appetites and target a deal appropriately

Scribble your stuff here

Week 18

Teams don't work - Everyone is different

We are all unique. We are all individuals. We are all geniuses.

So, why on earth do companies waste so much time and money trying to persuade people that they are just one of many? Or, that they need to work in exactly the same, strictly determined, manner? Or that being part of a team is the best thing since sliced bread?

It's rubbish. All of it. In fact, it is nonsense, daft, badly thought out and irritating too.

Teams don't work.

There is far too much emphasis on broad brushing everyone as part of a team these days. It's all high fives, pep talks and group problem solving. Along the way, the fact that everyone on that team is an individual and has their own unique strengths is suppressed, forgotten and cast aside. Is that a good thing? Of course it isn't.

People don't ever really empathise with their colleagues. Yes, everyone will get on well with a few people in the company, but I bet you a pound to a penny there will be others on the team who they really don't like. If you are honest, I bet you have a private bucket list of those who you think are absolutely not up to the job and those who are just so bloody lazy they don't ever pull their weight.

And you are going to go in there and offer everyone on the team a £1,000 bonus if the whole team achieves X target? How pleased is anyone going to be if they see a colleague who they don't rate, or who is totally lazy, getting £1,000 on the back of the rest of the firm's hard work? It's human nature to believe that if you do the hard work, then you should get the reward.

Yet, the accepted wisdom is that, like ants, if we all work together we can achieve anything, or at the very least, get the job done faster. That's just not true.

Just because you have a group of people working for you, does not mean they are a team. They are a group. That's it.

So, what's the answer? Treat people like individuals.

Think of it this way: a fish is great at swimming. That is their genius. Ask a fish to climb a wall though and they will just feel stupid. They can't do it. So, find the genius in each individual, nurture and encourage it, and you will have an office stuffed full of high achieving individuals. That is much more effective than shoehorning a bunch of people into a 'team' and expecting miracles.

To get a group to work to its optimum efficiency, the leader has to treat everyone as a person in their own right. Don't just go for collective solutions because it is the easy way out.

Get to know who you are dealing with, their strengths and weaknesses, and give them direction. Then:

- Educate. Often, people don't know their own genius. So, once you spot it, help them to develop it. This might mean moving them to a different position and teaching them skills. Sure, it will take a bit of time and patience, but they will love you to bits for it, love the company and be a loyal, committed, dedicated member of staff. Who wouldn't want a company stuffed full of people like this?

- Incentivise each person as an individual. If they do well, they will be rewarded.

- Celebrate success. Don't wait until the end of the year to grudgingly say, "Yeah, we all did well". Celebrate the small victories. When someone does something well, or has come up with a better, more efficient technique, or wins some new business, congratulate them. Loudly. Show them that their efforts are appreciated. You'd be amazed how energising this small act can be, yet it costs nothing to do.

If you encourage people to be individuals, they are far more likely to stand up and say, "Hey, wouldn't it be better if we did it like this? What if we looked at it backwards, or turned it inside out?" If you want to make your fortune and really stand out, that is what you need. Surround yourself with ideas people, deviants if you like, who are not afraid to stand up and be counted because what they are saying doesn't quite fit into a homogenous team culture.

Deviants are the difference between companies that produce something original and those that are merely average. They make things sparkle because deviants are the source of real innovation.

You, as a leader, have a key part in holding this all together. Obviously, you don't want a company stuffed full of bolshie people who all think they know better, just as you don't want a team of mediocre yes men and women. But, if you encourage an atmosphere of debate and enquiry and don't stamp on people who ask awkward questions, you will find a better way forward.

To achieve this, the person at the top should;

- Set out a clear direction. Poorly designed tasks, badly defined goals and an unclear agenda is a recipe for disaster. If you want to successfully lead a team of individuals, you have to make sure everyone knows where they need to end up. Unless the leader articulates a clear direction, there is a real risk their forward thinking deviants will pursue different agendas entirely.

- Direction is not the same as banging on about your 'vision' for the company. I guarantee you that, whatever the textbooks say, most people don't give a toss about your vision. It's your vision. They have their own vision. Your staff just want a good, happy, working environment, to know what you want to achieve, and to have someone who will listen to them when they have questions about it.

- Be approachable at all times. Don't lock yourself away in the office and hope things are going OK. Keep the door open. Walk around. Check. Make sure that if anyone wants to talk things through with you it is easy for them to do so. Be constantly supportive and give them the resources to do their jobs.

Most people believe that being a team player is the ultimate measure of a person's worth. It is not. There are many, many things that individuals can do much better if they are left to get on with it. This is particularly so if your organisation is involved in any sort of creative endeavour.

Your challenge as a leader is to manage a team of free-thinking individuals, set out a clearly defined direction and encourage everyone to question the status quo. It won't be easy, but the upsides are huge. And, believe me, it will be a lot better than trying to train a bunch of fish how to climb walls!

If you have a knowledge gap, make it your business to go understand it

Scribble your stuff here

Week 19

Precision networking

There can be few situations in business more annoying than getting a call or email like the following:

"Hi, Lyndon, it's Bryan Smith from Acme Industries. I don't know if you remember, but we met last year at that conference in Birmingham. I wonder if you can do me a favour....."

Put the phone down and walk away. Calls like this - and I get them all the time - go into top position by far on my networking 101. Bryan Smith and his ilk just don't get it.

Networking is an art. It produces vital contacts and can be invaluable to your business growth. But, get it wrong, and you'd be better off using your networking hours doing something useful. Like getting on a 'How to run my business properly' course.

Get out there. Meet as many useful people as you can. But stay in touch. That way, when the time comes when that person might actually come in useful, the person on the other end of the phone might be pleased to hear from you. Pleased to hear from you means happy to help.

Staying in touch means having a contact strategy. A contact strategy is a simple and highly effective way of keeping in touch. I am yet to come across anyone who has one or even talks about it, so you can have the edge on networking by having one. Here is how it works. After you have met a fellow business executive for the first time:

- Send an email or text that evening. Say something simple like, "Hi, it's Lyndon here, it was great to meet you today. We must have that coffee next time I am in London, or, if you are ever in my neck of the woods, give me a ring."

- Now contact has been made, the person at the other end of the communication will put your details into their phone.

- Follow up with another email or text one month later. It can be as simple as something like, "Hello John, how is business?"

- Your contact will usually reply and a conversation will begin. Away you go.

If I ever get a spare moment (and yes, we do all get them), I scroll through the contacts list on my smartphone. I make a mental note of who I haven't touched base with in a while and send them over a friendly greeting.

Then one day, when I see that my networking pal may be able to help me out or I can help him/her out with something, I can make contact without annoying the hell out of them. I've solved quite a lot of business problems with the help of my networking contacts simply by listening to their experiences.

After all, going to a networking event, or indeed any event, does not constitute networking. They're just beauty parades to help you decide who you are going to add to your network. It is what you do afterwards that counts.

There are plenty of other networking sins lining up for a place in my Room 101 too. Ignoring contacts and then demanding something out of the blue is not the only way people get networking completely wrong. In fact, in my view, the average businessperson commits a whole litany of errors while trying to create a useful network of contacts;

- They religiously attend dedicated 'networking events', but somehow fail to notice that, because everyone else there is doing the same thing, everyone is selling, nobody is buying.

- They are not discerning about the events they attend. A Rolodex full of nice networks and connections are all very nice, but it doesn't pay the bills. You need to meet potential clients, or people with expertise in areas you are lacking, not a bunch of people trying to flog you something.

- ....Which means you need to know what your goals are for networking in the first place. You know where your business is going, so don't waste time on making business connections for the sake of it.

- And, don't ever, ever pay to go to a 'networking event'. I see no need to shell out money for one when so much is available for free.

There are simple rules around networking. First and foremost, there is no such thing as a specific time and place for making contacts. You don't just work hard at building connections because there is a sign outside the door saying, 'This is a networking event'.

Networking can happen any time, anywhere and any place. All businesspeople should know how to meet other business people. It's what you do. So, why pay to be herded into a room with other people who don't know what they are doing either?

Secondly, ask yourself, "Why are you networking?" My purpose for networking is to meet other chief executives or owners of medium to large companies to obtain additional knowledge on specific areas of business. I may, for example, have an issue with technology and if I do, I want to be able to call on senior executives in the industry for their view. Thus, when I wanted to know more about monitoring my websites, I asked a contact from a multi-million dollar turnover American company for his help. My reasoning was that companies across the Atlantic were far in advance in this respect from UK players and I had, for some time, been cultivating US contacts with just this in mind. Sure enough, my main contact gave me some great pointers and recommended three companies stateside who would be able to help.

Thirdly, you, the business owner, should be doing the bulk of the networking. You are the only person who knows the strategy and goals of the business inside out, so it stands to reason that you should be making the contacts your company needs. It makes no financial sense to send your senior team off to all sorts of events which will only shore up their CVs and make them more visible on the jobs market. In the worse case scenario, they'll all go off to a network event together and spend the whole time chatting to their co-workers over free coffee and chocolate HobNobs. Encourage them to make and maintain business contacts, but don't let them do it at the expense of the day job.

The final golden rule to remember is that networking is a two-way process. It is not just about you. Just as any kid in the playground will tell you, if you don't share, you are not going to keep many pals. Once I have built a link with a contact (but not when I get an out-of-the-blue call from the Bryan Smiths of this world), I am always ready and willing to give any advice and help I can.

Networking can and will pay dividends, but it needs to be targeted and contacts must be maintained at all time. That is the key to precision networking.

Scribble your stuff here

Week 20

Dominate Distribution -
A slice of every cake

Distribution is, of course, how you get your product into the outstretched hands of the eager millions. In the old days, that pretty much meant producing your product and then getting it on to a shelf in a shop, or into the hands of a salesman or woman. This is now far from the case. Distribution is no longer a mundane process. Or, at least it shouldn't be. As an entrepreneur, you have a fantastic opportunity to seek out the most productive and innovative channels to get your goods sold to as many consumers as possible.

I'm always amazed when businesses don't regularly review their distribution processes. It's a great and relatively straightforward way to really expand your business. In its simplest form, all it means is identifying all the distribution channels you currently use, to see if you are providing your product into each one effectively.

In my own case, this is an exercise I regularly carry out. I look in minute detail at every aspect of my business. Over time, the modifications I have made include:

- Refining products suitable for insurance brokers. Insurance brokers are my competitors, but they can also provide business to me, as long as I give them products that their customers would like which helps them build their business.

- Developing an easy-to-use online business model for my constructaquote.com company for customers that like to buy on the internet.

- …..But, also providing an out-bound call centre for those who still like to talk to 'real' people.

Whichever way you cut it, I have almost maximised my distribution chain. That doesn't mean that I have sat back and rested on my laurels though; I still have more to do. I look at potential new channels all the time.

The type of distribution strategy you choose will depend very much on your industry, the type of product or service, and your business model, but all strategies could do with some scrutiny to see if they are really meeting the needs of all your customers. It may be time to refocus your efforts.

To see if you are servicing your customer case in the best way possible, it is well worth going back to basics and doing a market analysis. Most of you will have done some sort of analysis back when you started the business, particularly if you were applying for outside funding, but now is the time to do another one. I always do mine on a back of a cigarette packet and then act on it. Things in the modern world change all the time and thanks to the constant flow of new technology, the pace is faster than ever. Take a little time to do a thorough review now and you could discover a whole new sector of your market that is virtually untapped.

To begin with, get accurate figures on the size of the market and then segment the total number of potential customers by geographic factors, customer attributes, past preferences and trends.

Take a look at your competitors (after all, they will be looking to see what you do too). Check:

- How they are positioning themselves and where they currently distribute their products.

- What do your products have that your competitors don't?

- What specific needs do your products fulfil?

- Is there anything unique about them?

Never just copy your competitors.

Have a chat to your end customers too. They are, after all, best placed to voice their desires about new channels they'd rather use. Also, they'll give a good indication of the channels that are not working to optimum efficiency.

This process will give you plenty of clues on customer expectations about time and place of delivery. It should also reveal a handful of opportunity gaps if you are really on the ball.

Once you've answered these questions, you can start to imagine how else you could get your products to market. Are there any alternative channels that you have not considered that could give you a strategic advantage?

Some of the distribution channels you should be considering are:

- **Direct sales** - If you are not doing so already, selling directly to the consumer is usually the most cost effective distribution channel.

- **Manufacturer's representatives** - Manufacturer's reps, as they are known, are salespeople who work for agencies who handle an assortment of complimentary products. If you don't have capacity internally, this can be a cost effective solution.

- **Wholesale distributors** - The manufacturer sells to a wholesaler, who will sell it on to retailers or other agents, along a channel to the end-user.

- **Direct mail** - Selling to the end-customer through a direct mail campaign is nothing new, but are there opportunities for your goods that incorporate new media or social networking?

Once you've got all the information to hand, it is time to really get innovative. As always, I would give free reign to the wildest ideas and then work back from there. Some will work, and some won't, but if you don't give them an airing, you'll never know.

The sort of ideas you could come up with include:

- **Mobile delivery** - Could your products be loaded onto trucks and taken to where consumers are most likely to be (and willing to part with their cash)?

- **TV home shopping** - Does your product lend itself to an effective demonstration to promote its effectiveness? If so, TV shopping channels such as Home Delivery Network and QVC may be a great outlet.

- **Free trials** - If you are confident about your product (and it lends itself to it), why not offer free internet downloads? Consumers could trial it for a set number of days, and then if it works out well, could buy it outright.

These are just some examples to get you started - there are of course loads more possibilities. But, you won't get anywhere until you put distribution on the agenda. Literally.

Get your distribution right and it will add value to your product, as well as increasing its chances of getting in front of its intended consumer. That's well worth a look, isn't it?

Never have 3 people to do a 1 person job

Scribble your stuff here

Week 21

Social Frenzy

Ask anyone in business about social media and they will tell you if you are not 'in', you are most certainly out. "Great," you'll say, "what's in it for me?" That is where the conversation will usually grind to a halt. Everyone thinks it is a good thing, but no one quite knows why. In the frenzy to get signed up and get our innermost thoughts out to an eager public, not many people seem to have given much thought about what it can actually do for them.

That sort of wishy washiness is not good enough for a fortune hunter. We need to deal with certainties. There isn't enough time for anything else.

So, let me dispel a few myths:

- Twitter, Facebook et al will not guarantee you a single sale or referral. Not one.

- Just because you are doing it, doesn't mean that anyone is looking. And, unless you do it properly, they probably aren't.

- Building up an army of followers is not enough. Bully for you, you have friends, so what? You need to engage with them if you want to get any value out of it.

- Social media cannot, at a stroke, replace all your marketing efforts and save you thousands of pounds.

Or, if it makes it any easier:

If you are a fortune hunter there is absolutely no value whatsoever telling all and sundry that you are in your garden drinking cappuccino.

(Apart from the fact that you shouldn't be wasting time sitting around relaxing if you are really serious about making real money.)
So, listen carefully and I will answer the question about how you get the most out of social media:

- Think WIIFM? (What's in it for me?) - If the aim of the game is to convert your social media followers into paying customers or business associates, give them a reason to want to do business with you. That reason should usually be a benefit to them. So, for example, I will regularly tweet the latest unemployment or insurance statistics, so I am seen as a useful source of information. Alternatively, contests and competitions are a great way to engage followers. If you tie them in with your business and offer a prize that means something to your target audience, you'll get results.

- Add value. WIIFM isn't just about adding value to your personal posts. If you submit a link, add some value by including a really good description of the article. Better still, tell everyone why it is worth their while reading it. Go one step further by adding your opinion of what the author left out and why you would have said something more. It's a great way to build up a weighty profile for yourself.

- Consumers into customers. Social media does not, as I said, automatically get you customers. But, if you provide engaging and informative text, it will get you a lot of consumer followers. Keep that up and, over time, some of those consumers will turn into customers. Don't be afraid to ask for the sale once you've built up a relationship too. If you repeat your call to action regularly, and accompany it with lots of great content and information, people will bite.

- Build relationships. Next time someone becomes your virtual friend, or follows you, don't just send out the standard 'thanks for following' message, or worse not acknowledge them at all. Take a moment to see who this person is on the other side of the internet connection. Ask yourself how you could help them in a meaningful way. Better still, ask them. Then, just as with networking in the 'real' world, keep in touch and send them a link with some information now and again.

- Social first, media second. Don't be dull. Provide a sense of enjoyment and fun in your communications. If you show your true personality, people will want to be a part of what you are doing and keep up with what you are saying. It is after all social media. I recently tweeted that I had taken my son to see Fast and Furious Five, adding a postscript that my prized Mustang car was for sale on Piston Heads. I had six enquiries within minutes. I could have easily have tweeted, "I want to sell my Mustang for £x". However, by tying in the sale of my American car with an American action film, I got the right people's attention.

- Focus. It's pretty easy to sign up to the various sites on offer, but that is not enough. Unless you put in some work, you won't get a lot out of it. For a kick-off, limit the number of sites you are on - if you are running a busy business you don't have time to waste on things that have no real value. Once you decide what does have some value, commit to it and give it some attention. Keep your profile up-to-date, maintain an active presence and keep in touch.

- Diversify. Taking into account the above point, don't limit yourself to too few sites either. Different sites have different strengths. I've always found LinkedIn very useful for professional and new business contacts, Digg is better suited to news, particularly technology and weird stuff, and Twitter is great for broader issues.

- Give. Anthropologists call it reciprocity. It basically means if you do something nice for someone else, then they'll do the same for you. It is basic human nature. If you want recommendations on LinkedIn, then you need to start doing some yourself. If you want people to follow you on Twitter, then you need to do it too. Take the lead and people will return the favour.

- Don't neglect other channels. Do the maths. I'll bet you get a thousand times ROI (return on investment) from your dull old email contacts list than from your Twitter followers. Don't neglect them because you are too busy playing with the new 'in' crowd. It is a dangerous game.

Social media sites are a great way to promote your business, find contacts and build relationships, but they don't just work all by themselves. You've got to put in some effort too, because it is a tool, not a machine. As with all tools, you've got to play your part and provide them with the necessary energy to get them working effectively, not just sit back and wait for them to work miracles. You only get out of it what you put into it. Keep these principles in mind and, pretty soon, people will respond.

Focus on your core and build it

Scribble your stuff here

Week 22

Social Frenzy - Part two - 50 quick fire ideas to give your tweets a boost

As we saw in the last entry, social media can be a great, low-cost, way to promote your business. For those fortune hunters who are still confused about where to get started, or even those who are already regular tweeters but always on the look out for good ideas, I'm listing 50 quick-fire tips on how to give your tweets a boost. And, to keep within the theme, I've restricted each one to 140 characters or less.

First some basics:

1. Make sure your personal profile is up-to-date - first impressions are critical for would-be followers.
2. Add a picture of yourself. Your followers want to see you.
3. When you talk about your company, make it useful. Give advice, blog posts, links and pictures.
4. If promoting a blog post, explain what's coming, don't just dump the link.
5. Tweet about other people's posts. It'll give you a new angle and show you are not just "that guy from Blogg Co".
6. Make sure you don't miss a thing by following your competitors.
7. Get others in the company to tweet too. It'll add some variety.
8. Post questions for some quick answers and answer others' questions to establish your credibility.
9. Create links to your website or blog, but don't over do it.
10. Add your Twitter feed to your blog or other social media profiles.
11. Steer clear from the 'cappuccino in the garden' posts, but do show a human side by posting pictures and personal comments.
12. The more you tweet, the more people will get to know you and your company.

Ideas on what to tweet:

13. Don't think in terms of "What are you doing?" Answer the question, "What has your attention?"
14. Stay on top of any news that will affect your industry.
15. Provide an enticing, must-click, description of a good article.
16. Ask questions. Twitter is a great medium for getting opinions.
17. Heck - Twitter can make a great, and instant, opinion poll.
18. Use it to break news about your firm. It works much faster than traditional sources.
19. Direct attention towards good things that you have done - or are about to do.

20. Show you are at the centre of things at industry events by giving real-time updates.
21. Ensure a portion of your tweets are nothing to do with your type of business. It will add some value.

Get more from others' tweets

22. Twitter gives you an hourly opportunity to learn something new if you look for it and follow the right people.
23. Find out what your customers really think of you - and then act on it if it's not good news.
24. Engage - have conversations.
25. Build relationship, not just business connections.
26. Make introductions between your connections who may benefit from knowing each other. They may do the same back.

Some useful etiquette

27. Follow interesting people. If someone tweets something interesting, see who they follow and follow them too.
28. Commenting on others' tweets and retweeting is a great way to build a community.
29. Don't blow your own trumpet too much. People don't like it when others are too full of themselves.
30. If you can't resist a bit of self-promotion, balance it by bigging up others too.
31. Always be positive. There is nothing more off-putting than someone constantly complaining or being negative.
32. Be original. People don't like regurgitated content, or to keep seeing the same stuff time and time again.
33. Share links to some great things in your industry (it doesn't matter that you didn't think of them).
34. If someone says you are using Twitter wrong, ignore them. They can unfollow if they don't like how you are using it.

Some helpful techie stuff:

35. If you want a RT (retweet), leave at least 15 characters to give the RTer space so they don't shorten your message.
36. Put 'PLS RT' (please retweet) if you want a RT - the old fashioned call to action does work.
37. RT others often. What goes around…
38. 'TweetLater' is really useful because it lets you to schedule your tweets.
39. It also allows you to receive email digests of keyword activity in the Tweetosphere. Use it to track trends.
40. TwitterFox, a Firefox web browser plug-in, lets you view Tweets within your web browser as a pop-up menu. Very handy.
41. Ping.fm allows you to post updates across ALL of your social media sites in one single step.
42. Twitter for Facebook lets you forward your updates direct to your Facebook as a status update.
43. Hellotxt posts text and media to separate accounts on multiple social networks and publishing platforms.

Don't get Tweet fatigued!

44. You don't have to read every tweet.
45. Use direct messages for one-to-one conversations if there is no value in what you are saying to those in Twitter at large.
46. There is no need to reply (or feel guilty about not replying) to every @ tweet directed to you.
47. Focus and commit. Devote at least half an hour per day to discovering and tweeting...
48. But, don't tweet at the expense of using your time to represent clients or do paying work.
49. Schedule specific times and treat tweet sessions like you would a meeting.
50. Stick with it to build a campaign. Don't try once, criticise it and never go back. The benefit will build over time.

Your use of Twitter may vary according to whatever business you are in, but there can be no argument that used well, it can be a real asset to your marketing efforts. These tips will help you get started. Given time though, you'll probably have plenty of your own ideas to add.

Diversify only when you have dominated your core market

Scribble your stuff here

Week 23

Marketing your Online Business

When I finally got around to building my first website, I was pretty pleased with myself. True, I had pontificated for a while, but I had gone ahead and spent £20,000 to build it.

The year was 1996 and it was early days in the dotcom boom. I had read all the hype, firmly believed it and fancied I was going to make a fortune overnight. True, my website was a bit rough around the edges and a tad clunky by today's standards, but that didn't dent my confidence for a moment because it was top notch for the time.

When the actual website launched, I was so proud I thought I might burst. There it was, online. I could see it, click around it and it worked just fine. I sat back and waited for the orders to come flooding in. And waited. And waited. The weeks passed by and absolutely nothing happened. Not a thing. Not one enquiry. Zip, nada, nix.

By this time, I was getting quite panicky. I had, after all, spent £20,000 which was no mean sum. I couldn't really afford to spend that money.

What had I done wrong? Well, I had made the most basic of mistakes. I had failed to tell anyone about my new online venture. Sure, I had mentioned it on my letterhead but that was about as far as it went. I had simply continued to market my firm in the traditional way via direct mail and phone calls.

Years later in 2005, I launched my current website, constructaquote.com and this time, I engaged experts to help me with the marketing. The cost was pretty staggering - £120,000 a year for three years - but I learned a hell of a lot. My site is hugely successful and has indeed earned me my fortune.

My advice to anyone who is considering an online business is to engage some sort of expert help with the marketing. Yes, it will cost you a lot of money, although it does not have to cost anywhere near £120,000, but it will also make you a considerable amount of money too.

Before you do this though, I would make a point of finding out as much as you can first, so you can find the right agency and have some input into the decisions that are made. I certainly had to kiss a few frog-like agencies, until I found the prince that transformed my online business and I believe that if I had known more to begin with, I could have made the whole process a lot easier and more cost effective. So, before you spend any money:

1. Think carefully about the look of your website. Your online service is the window into your business. It is an important part of your brand and a bad site will give a bad impression. Forget about trying to be too cool though. As a rule of thumb, the more sophisticated you try to be and the more bells and whistles you try to add, the more likely it is to create problems for the user. Some browsers may not work well with your website if it is too complex.

2. Make it fast and easy for customers to order. A site with a difficult sales process will lose you customers who get frustrated and go elsewhere. Make it easy to search for things too.

3. Get the best domain name you can afford. It should be short, easy to remember and reflect what your business actually does. This is what your customers will remember you by.

4. Consider paid advertising for your site such as Pay Per Click or Google Ad Words, but take care to understand the process before you commit. All the major search engines offer you the ability to buy ads based on certain keywords of your choice. Your ad will be displayed when the would-be customer keys in their search. However, this facility comes at a price - and if you don't have the right keywords, you could be wasting your money. There are some cost effective agencies that can help you with this.

5. Consider carefully the keywords you put in your header page, even if you are not choosing the paid ad option above. Write a descriptive title, rich in about five to eight keywords that people will probably use to find you. This is what will appear in search engines when your page is found.

6. Make sure your H1, H2 and H3 tags are in place. Search engines consider keywords that appear in the headline and also in the sub-heads (H2 and H3) and use them to identify your site as an authority. Make sure your desired keywords and phrases appear in one or more header. Provide as many clues to search engines as you can.

7. Create a site map. A site map page which lists all the relevant pages on your website helps search engines - and visitors - find all your pages. This is particularly important if it's a large site. Also, make sure it is updated as the site grows.

8. Link build. Don't pay for link services - search engines are on to this - but it is well worth trying to build up a strategy where other relevant sites link to yours. You can do this by building a site which offers something valuable or unique to people, so they are not only coming to you because it is a purely commercial site. You could offer some great articles, or resources, for example, which could be a real help to your potential customers.

9.   Let your customers do some of the work. A happy customer is a great asset. Make sure there are facilities for customers to share their positive experiences with social sharing buttons. Actively encourage people to spread the word about the business by adding a message to your email confirmations and at the end of articles.

10.   Update your website regularly. No one likes a static site and that goes for search engines too.

Don't forget to promote your business every time you go online. If you take part in online forums, include a signature line at the end of any comments you make, which provide a link back to your site. Target forums which link back to the product or service that you sell and never miss an opportunity to establish yourself as an expert in your field.

The most important thing about an online site is to establish regular traffic. As I found to my cost early on, there is little point having a great website if no one knows about it. Get help if you need it, but make sure you know enough to get the right help.

Then, make it happen!

Spot the difference in your superior competitors

Scribble your stuff here

www.diaryofafortunehunter.com
Follow me on twitter@lyndonx

Week 24

Let's do PR!

I first instructed a PR agent back in 2002. I wanted help with profile building because I was fed up with having to explain to suppliers who I was, who my company were and what we did. My brief to the agency was to raise the profile of Moorhouse Insurance, particularly among the trade. Sure enough, after a period of time (well, about seven months), I no longer had to explain myself. I even started getting the slightly disconcerting experience of people coming up to me at trade events and saying, "Hi Lyndon!" That's always a bit weird when you have never met someone before in your life.

Unfortunately, my experience with PR agencies has not always been as satisfactory. Some time after my earlier public relations triumph, I appointed another larger agency to raise our profile among our end-users, although I still retained our original agency for trade press. The agency I chose made a glitzy presentation and promised me the earth. I was a little sceptical, but decided to give them a trial.

I carefully set down what I expected each month for their not insubstantial fee and they eagerly agreed to do it all and more.

Month one passed and things looked pretty good. They achieved everything they said they would do and I started to feel quite hopeful. Then, in month two, they only managed to deliver what they had set up in month one.

"What's happening?" I asked. "This isn't nearly as much as I was expecting. In fact, it isn't even close to what we agreed."

"But we've got you national press coverage!" the agency's account director exclaimed, as though I was clearly expecting too much.

The next month was not much better. I reminded them several times what I was expecting, but my pleas seemed to fall on deaf ears. Needless to say, I cancelled the trial early and went elsewhere. My argument was that, yes, they had achieved what I wanted in month one, but they appeared to expect two months' payment for their endeavours, despite what we had previously agreed.

I have always prided myself on being a man of principle and high standards. If I say I will achieve X for a client, I will always go out of my way to achieve X, and Y too. I won't stand for complacency and ignorance, and nor should you. You are, after all, investing your hard-earned fortune in services like this, and should never expect second best.

I will, however, add that I have had some very good service from PR companies in the past. Overall, it has been well worth the investment because it has built up a high degree of recognition of my businesses and this in turn has played an important part in boosting sales.

My view is, as an entrepreneur, you have to go into a relationship with a PR company with both eyes open. The most important things I have learnt along my PR journey are:

1. **Choose your agency carefully.** It is well worth investing time and trouble in making sure you get the right PR company on board. Don't fall for fancy offices, impressive client lists, and lots of bluff and bluster. Find out if they really do what they say they'll do. I'd go as far as speaking to some of their existing clients to see if they are happy with the service they are getting. Make sure too that your prospective agency has some knowledge about your industry - you don't want to pay for their time while they get up to speed. It also helps if a PR company has some journalistic experience among its key staff, so they understand what makes a good story and how to approach editors.

2. **Agree terms, conditions and specifics up front.** As per my example earlier, it is much easier when everyone knows what is expected from them from the off. If you are paying a monthly retainer, get in writing exactly what this covers on a month-by-month basis. Then, make sure you are always getting what you pay for. Every month. If you find that your PR firm is spending an inordinate amount of time on planning and research, flag it up immediately. You want less planning and more doing.

3. **Define what you consider to be success and measure the results.** Your PR campaign is not a giant ego trip to make you look better. Make sure that you have a specific purpose in mind and share it with your agency. Then, measure the results against it.

4. **Manage the process.** The best results come when the PR campaign is driven by you. You know the best stories about your business and the burning issues in your sector. (If you don't, you are real trouble - but that is nothing to do with PR) Never let the PR company be the sole generator of ideas. Plan your campaign as much as you can by scheduling in advance items you can tell the world about.

5. **Be available.** Just because you have appointed a PR company does not mean your job is done. Make sure you are always available to journalists to comment on a story - even if it has not been generated by you and is about another company in your sector. Journalists love it when they know they have a good industry contact who will always respond to their requests and help them with urgent gaps in their story. Build relationships across the media and always return telephone calls from reporters straight away. It, of course, helps if you keep up-to-date with the issues in your sector, so you can always give an informed and intelligent opinion. Be the expert in your field.

6. **Tell everyone about it!** Don't forget that PR is an internal as well as an external exercise. If your company is getting good press (or indeed any press) flag it up to the team. It'll help motivate them and show them that they are part of a company that is going places. (See 'Week 14: Good Drivers', for other tips on motivation). Ask your PR company for other ideas on an internal PR strategy too.

PR is just like any other service you buy in for your business and you must make equally sure that you get an adequate return on your investment. The only way that will happen is if you are very clear about what you want, when you want it and are prepared to do your bit to make it happen.

Don't be afraid to have high expectations, just as you do with all the aspects of your business. PR can and will have a significant impact, if you follow these steps. It will help get your company more widely known too. Just make sure your standards are as exacting as with the rest of your activities. Oh, and prepare yourself for an increasing amounts of chats with strangers who recognise you from the media.

Greatness comes with great efforts

Scribble your stuff here

www.diaryofafortunehunter.com
Follow me on twitter@lyndonx

Week 25

Relationships and being your own brand champion

It's always a shock when you meet someone, think you've got on pretty well with them and then it turns out they can't stand the sight of you. It's even worse when that person takes such an active dislike to you that they subsequently feel duty-bound to regularly disparage you behind your back to anyone who will listen. The worst scenario of all is when this happens in a business setting. Not only is this upsetting on a personal level, it can also be downright damaging professionally.

This happened to me around 15 years ago with a guy from my industry who I once thought I got on well with. For no apparent reason, he made it his life's mission to slate me in the marketplace at any and every opportunity. I lost count of the times that people would relate to me some scandalous, and completely false, tale that this guy had peddled about me. I was utterly at a loss as to why someone, even if he was a competitor, would do something like this. But he did, and he went on doing it.

The experience made me reflect deeply on what people said about me and my business. Although there seemed to be little I could immediately do about my erstwhile friend, short of taking out an injunction or punching his lights out (I considered both options), I resolved to get as many people as I could around me saying good things.

The important point to remember here is, while you can and should get an outside PR consultancy to spread the word (for advice on how to manage this process see the previous week's entry; Let's do PR), the best advocate for you and your company is you. The one role in your firm that you cannot afford to leave unfilled is that of brand champion and brand guardian to your business.

Think about it - the most successful brands in the world have a figurehead who continuously advocates them. When you see a picture of Richard Branson, you immediately think Virgin. Bill Gates brings Microsoft to your mind, and when you see Mark Zuckerberg, you think Facebook.

If you are building a business, you should be thinking this way from the start. You need to constantly consider both your brand and your business brand. It doesn't matter what size you are now, you need to lay the foundation for the future. The more people you get saying good things about your company, the less that outsiders will believe if (or when) jealous competitors attempt to undermine you. I think my experience with the fellow who bad-mouthed me is unusual - but the point about the importance of building a rock solid brand is no less valid.

My strategy to get people talking about and saying good things about my business is relatively simple.

This is what I do:

1.   When I meet new people I make sure I am polite, professional and friendly.

2.   I always try to slip some information about myself and my business into our conversation in a lively and interesting way. However, I also make sure that I listen as much as I talk in order to show that I am interested in their opinion about what I am saying and also in what they do themselves.

3.   I make it a priority to highlight any recent successes in my corporate life, because it is human nature to like dealing with successful people.

4.   I make sure I keep in touch after the meeting via text, or email, or the odd phone call, just to see how they are (see 'Week 19: Precision networking', for more tips on how to do this effectively).

5.   If anyone I meet asks for my help or advice on either a professional or personal matter, I always respond quickly and do my best to direct them towards a satisfactory solution. If I have agreed to do anything to move things forward, I ensure that I deliver on my promises.

6.   I maintain a positive appearance at all times and ensure that I speak positively about people in my industry.

By doing all of these things at every opportunity, I have succeeded in building my business into a strong, respected, brand. Along the way I have sealed a number of solid, meaningful, relationships with people who have been of great help to me in the commercial world. These contacts are from all levels of the industry and I never discriminate by going for the 'big' names and ignoring more junior executives. Again, this has stood me in good stead, because you never truly know who the real rising stars are. Indeed, on a number of occasions, a lower level executive who I have formed a good working relationship with, has gone on to become chief executive of some quite sizeable companies. Now, that is a useful relationship to have!

Now, if like me, you like to cut to the chase and find out what happens at the end of a story, you are probably wondering what became of the fellow who seemed out to destroy me. Well, there is a curious ending to this tale.

After spending many years simultaneously building up my business and the profile of my brand, I pretty much felt that I had put the incident behind me. I occasionally got reports of this fellow's sniping, but now that my profile was so good, I ignored it.

Then, I was at a large industry awards ceremony and I came within a few feet of him. My immediate thought was if he tried anything, or attempted to talk to me, I might very well break all my personal rules and deck him. I suppressed this urge, as it is not my way, but was amazed when he walked right up to me.

What happened next surprised me even more.

Looking very sheepish and red in the face, the man extended his hand.

"I would like to profusely apologise for what I have been saying over the past ten years," he said. "I have no idea why I did it and know I had no right or grounds to do it either. I am so very sorry."

At least this chap finally had the guts to apologise for his extraordinary behaviour and was prepared to do it in front of colleagues in the industry. I immediately made the decision to forgive him and move on. I had had my day and he had had his big embarrassment.

I don't pretend to understand why he did what he did. The lesson that I, and indeed you, can learn from this odd episode is that it is never a good thing to slate anyone, especially your competitors, and that anything that doesn't kill you can make you stronger. Concentrate on building your brand, prove the naysayers wrong and you will always triumph in the end.

The more people you speak to, the more successful you become

Scribble your stuff here

Week 26

Real Approach to Business - Choosing and working with paid advisors

When your business gets to a certain size, you will suddenly become very popular. Overnight, consultants of every sort from the pure 'management' type, to experts in HR, to sales gurus, will come knocking at your door offering to deliver theory to you and your staff for a handsome fee.

My bank manager even had a pop at this after I had been in business for five years.

"You are growing too fast," he declared solemnly. Then he added, in all seriousness, "I can help you take things at a slower, more sensible, pace."

This sort of nonsense drives me crazy. I know my business and what it needs far better than anyone either on the inside or the outside. If I need help, or to increase my learning in an unfamiliar field, I will ask for it. I certainly don't want to be 'sold' a service I don't need from someone who is clearly unqualified to give it.

Slow down my growth indeed? I ask you.

This is not an out-and-out rebuttal of consultants. I have, in recent years, engaged outside help on a large project. In this case, I wanted to create bespoke training programmes for my business and decided that I needed experts to guide me on the finer points of delivering the right products and skills.

I chose my consultants carefully, worked with them closely and, as is my way, learned a great deal from the experience. Although I was happy with the result I got, I could see that there is a lot of scope for the consultant/client relationship to go wrong.

For a kick-off, while there are a million books, websites and college course on how to become a consultant, there is pretty much nothing pointing the other way i.e. how do you choose, work with and get the best out of your outside expert?

This is pretty essential information because consultants, as everybody knows, don't come cheap. Hopefully no one would give you such ludicrous advice such as stop growing your business, but it is easy to see how you could get pushed in completely the wrong direction.

So, in a bid to help my fellow fortune hunters not get distracted by those repeated knocks on the door, here is my guide to choosing and getting the best out of your consultants.

1. **Ask yourself; do you really need a consultant?** It is an obvious first question, but no less important in the asking. Make sure you are not doing this because you have been persuaded into it because of a powerful sales pitch following that knock on the door. If there is a problem in the business that needs solving, look at other sources of help too. There is lots of free help out there from friends, business owners, forums, social networks and so on. Keep your cash and grow your business.

2. **Be totally clear on the purpose, scope and objectives of what you are trying to do.** It stands to reason that if you don't know where you are going, any path will take you there. Plus, if you don't lay out exactly what you want, it gives a consultant carte blanche to tell you what you want. Once you get into that sort of scenario, it's odds on that the advisor will place their interests ahead of yours. And, they'll charge you for the pleasure too.

3. **Work the way that you want to work.** Engaging an advisor is just the same as taking on any other external service (See 'Week 24: Let's do PR!'). You should define the hours you want them to work, how they will be reimbursed and the results you expect. Draft a schedule for the completion date of each goal during the project, even down to a specific day of the week. Structure your approach to give you the level of control you desire, and add in a quick and easy exit strategy if things don't go to plan.

4. **Be a little flexible.** Most consultancies worth their fee will have worked for a wide range of companies across a range of disciplines. They will have a whole bunch of tried and tested ways of getting things done. If you trust your consultant and think they know what they are doing (and you should - otherwise you shouldn't have signed them up) it is well worth listening to their recommendations with an open mind. There is no point hiring an advisor to advise you to keep everything the way it is, or simply to tell you what you want to hear. Likewise, you need a consultant that is flexible to the ever-growing needs of you, the client. Set out at the planning stage (see point 2) that both sides are open to hearing any wild, yet potentially valid, ideas that crop up and how you would agree to go forward from there. If you haven't allowed for this, that is how conflicts begin.

5. **Manage the process.** Put your best people onto the task (they may learn something too) and make sure that there is plenty of feedback throughout the process. Let the consultants know what they are doing well and what, if anything, isn't meeting your expectations. If there is a team working with your firm, make sure that you, as the boss, are in direct contact with the senior consultant so they can handle any sensitive issues quickly and efficiently if and when they come up.

Getting the best out of your relationship with a consultant really does come down to setting out expectations on both sides, right at the start. Conflicts only ever arise if the assumptions on either side are different from what the other originally anticipated.

If you get the relationship right before you begin work, consultants can offer you a great way to introduce some new thinking into the business and free your time to do something more productive elsewhere.

The important thing is to never allow yourself, or your business, to be ruled by any consultant, however impressive their credentials. It is down to you to drive the business and its components forward. There is no point in paying someone else to deliver half of what you could do yourself while interrupting your core skills to boot. As I said, keep your cash and grow your business.

Act local, think global

Scribble your stuff here

Week 27

Take a Moment - Don't let opportunities pass you by

Every now and then, something special will happen to you and your business. This special moment may present itself by design, or it might emerge because of circumstances, or even a combination of the two. The crucial factor is - do you recognise and seize the opportunity? Or, are you so wrapped up in your day-to-day business that you let opportunities slip by one by one? Or, worse still, do you simply fail to recognise how good an opportunity is when you do see one?

Opportunities present themselves in a number of different ways. You may have negotiated a great price on a product that you sell, or have designed an unbeatable product line. Suddenly, something you thought would do OK goes flying off the shelves. Alternatively, perhaps a whole new market or technology is opening up in your sector. Some new kids on the block may be fiddling around on the edges, but only a company with scale or know-how like yours can take it to the next level. There are dozens of other potential sources of opportunities besides.

Often the window to maximise an opportunity is short, maybe only a matter of months. It could be just weeks.

What do you do then?

You take a moment.

I don't mean sit back for so long that you let your opportunity sail by. I mean, stop for a moment, think about what you have got and work out a clever strategy to maximise your profit at the earliest possible moment.

I've learned from bitter experience the cost of not doing this. About 14 years ago, when I was fairly new to the insurance market, I put together an idea for an online comparisons insurance business to compliment my bricks and mortar firm. It was at a time when hardly any companies had cottoned on to the potential for selling insurance products online and no one had done a comparison site, especially for small businesses.

Back then, I had a lot of other things on my plate and kept putting off doing anything concrete about my online idea. There was always something else more pressing that needed sorting out. Looking back, I think I wasted a lot of time. Obviously I did eventually get around to it four years later and it was a great success, but I could have got there a lot quicker and could have got a lot bigger if I had stopped for a moment, properly weighed up what I had and then got on with it.

I call an opportunity like my putative online insurance business a 'Hot Money' moment. In the right environment, a hot money moment can build your profits rapidly without adding a whole lot of cost. Plus, if the opening seems that good, it may even be worth committing to add cost as a percentage of incremental income to max out your gain. The point is, if you have a possible hot money idea, you should definitely be giving it some headroom.

There are three stages to capturing a great opportunity. The first is to obviously spot it in the first place and I have already put some ideas down about that in Week 2 and 3: The Next Big Thing. The world is clearly full of great possibilities, but spotting them is not simply a question of being in the right place at the right time (although that always helps).

Knowing which are the right ones for you requires constant alertness, continuous scanning of the marketplace and an openness to accept new ideas, however off the wall they may seem at first. If you are doing this, you will ensure that nothing passes you by before you get a chance to properly analyse it.

Once you have spotted something that might be a goer, now is your cue to take a moment and properly assess its potential. All opportunities are different, but the six questions you should be giving serious attention to are:

1. Are you the right person to make this happen and do you have the right team around you to do it?

2. Have you got the right resources to build this opportunity up from? Or will you be starting from scratch? If so, is that currently possible?

3. Is there really a good market for this great opportunity? How much do you know about it? Has it been tested?

4. Can any of the companies you currently work with be of use? Or do you have to access an entirely new supply base?

5. Are your current processes sufficient to get this idea off the ground? If you incorporate this opportunity into your existing model, could it jeopardise your core business?

6. Do you have the funding, or access to it, that you would need to get this off the ground or scale it?

Each one of these questions is critical to bringing your opportunity to life. It is vital that you give each one attention and think it through properly.

The final stage of realising an opportunity is, of course, making it happen. If you have taken your moment and worked methodically through the above six questions, execution is generally pretty straightforward. When plans fail to get off the ground, it is usually down to one or two crucial parts of the puzzle being forgotten, badly thought through, or deliberately ignored. You may have to make the odd adjustment as you go along, but as long as you have taken the time to consider the variables from the six areas above, you should be in pretty good shape to make the most of your opportunity.

Being in a good position to max out the benefit of any opportunity at a blink of an eye is what every business owner strives for. Or at least they should do. So, take a full stop every now and again, and devote your energies into analysing all the opportunities you have at your fingertips, what you need to do to make them happen, and what strategies you will use to make them the success they deserve to be.

Take your moment - it could be the best thing you do today.

If it works, use it

Scribble your stuff here

www.diaryofafortunehunter.com
Follow me on twitter@lyndonx

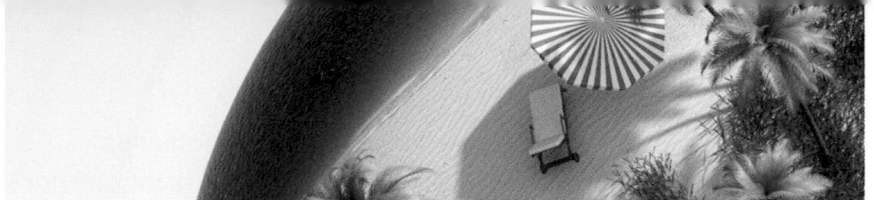

Week 28

Diversify or not? Great ideas to expand your business with minimal risk

To diversify, or not diversify, that is the question. Or is it? One of the most challenging decisions an entrepreneur is faced with is whether to branch out into an entirely new area. It is an unpredictable and high stakes game, which can turn out to be one of the riskiest strategies of all.

The corporate world is littered with the remnants of misguided diversifications, and even our most successful business giants are not immune from the diversification bug. Did you know, for example, that fast food giant McDonald's branched out into hotels in the late 1990s? Probably not, because if you blinked you'll have missed the short-lived Golden Arch hotels in Switzerland.

The problem is, an entrepreneur's strength is also their greatest weakness. They can't stop coming up with a stream of amazing new business ideas. Just when everything is running along OK, they can't help thinking, "Wouldn't it be great if I started another business doing X or Y?" Before you know it, they will have set off in an entirely new direction.

(Just to clarify, because there are many misunderstandings about diversification, by diversification, I mean launching into an entirely new industry, not simply a new product for your core market. Diversification is a different business model, selling a completely new product, to a completely new market, via a completely new company.)

Diversification and expansion is a subject I have been thinking about a lot lately. For a while, I was really torn.

On the one hand, I don't like to quell my natural entrepreneurial exuberance, which is fuelled by coming up with, and trialling, big new ideas. However, on the other, if I put all my energies (and cash) into starting something completely new, I could easily erode the value of my core business.

Although I am constantly coming up with schemes for new ventures, I have taken a deliberate decision to steer clear. On a purely financial basis, it just doesn't make sense for me. Right now, I know that if I consider an investment of, say, £100,000 in a new venture, it could very well take as much as £500,000 off the value of my business if I decide to sell it within the next 12 months (If you are not sure how I worked that out - as a rough rule of thumb, the value of your firm is five times your profit). If I took £100,000 off the bottom line to invest in my diversified business and it had not yet realised its potential by the time I came to sell, that would come straight off my core firm's value; £100,000 x 5 = £500,000.

However, at the same time, I do need to find a way to fulfil my natural entrepreneurial spirit and maintain my motivation, without eroding the value of my potential or hypothetical exit. (For tips on motivation, see Week 35: Go looking for trouble - Staying motivated.)

How could I maintain my interest, without being tempted to diversify? Strangely enough, when I stopped bubbling over with thoughts of how I could do things better elsewhere, I could see I was missing a lot of opportunities in my own core sector.

I asked myself the basic question; what could my company do better than any of its competitors in the current market? I was amazed at the number of answers I came up with.

One of my solutions was to launch Moorlife, a life insurance business which capitalised on all my knowledge in the industry and gave me a new venture to get my teeth into. It was a new sector of my industry, but complimentary to the rest of my business. Sure enough, the business boomed overnight.

Another new venture was to scale up in the van insurance market. In the past, this side of the business had just ticked along, but I noticed that, almost without effort, the number of enquiries we were getting from van insurance was soaring. So, I recruited 20 new people and started experimenting with aggregator software to offer customers in this market the best possible deal. I also made sure that my company had enough additional income streams, such as roadside recovery and legal expenses policies, so we could generate more income from this growing segment. Sure enough, we went from writing an average of £30,000 a month in policies to roughly six times that, almost overnight. All because I changed the focus on my main business.

Now, I could have answered my entrepreneurial calling by going into running a human resources company, or a voucher code business, or a publishing operation. These are all businesses I have had ideas on (and some of them quite forward-thinking!). However, I took the decision to re-channel that entrepreneurial spirit and fulfil that start-up excitement I crave by concentrating my energies on beefing up my core business. Looking at the numbers, I am glad I did.

I believe that this thought process would help any entrepreneur who is considering where to go next and whether they should expand or diversify.

The key to successful diversification in your sector is to be able to determine the exact parameters of your industry and your own core competencies. If your definition of your market is too broad-brush, such as "We're in the entertainment business" or "in electronics", all sorts of problems can creep in. Blue Circle, one of the world's biggest cement producers, famously diversified into waste management, gas stoves and even lawnmowers in the 1980s. Apparently, the logic behind the lawnmowers was based on the fact that you "need a lawnmower for your garden which, after all, is next to your house".

Once you lose focus like this, you are in a bad way. If diversification and expansion is on your mind, consider carefully the nature of your company's strategic assets, core industry and how you can best take advantage of what you already have. Most business owners usually only think of diversification because their core business is not doing as well as they would like and they think going into something different will boost their profits…. Wrong!

My view is you are generally better off sticking to your knitting. The only time you should consider something entirely new is when you have absolutely exhausted the market you are in, or have developed a position of such market dominance that you have no alternative than diversify, or growth will grind to a halt. If you have not saturated the market you are in, or are nowhere near doing so, you will be wasting your time, and putting your core business in danger too if you wander off in another direction. It will simply distract you and take up valuable brain space.

If it's not broken, find a break and fix it

Scribble your stuff here

Week 29

Hypergrowth - Stepping up the pace

In a business, there is growth and then there is hypergrowth. Any fortune hunter's plan should include visions for at least one period of hypergrowth, or clearly they are not really serious about making it big.

For those who haven't come across the term, hypergrowth involves rapidly scaling up a business, aiming for exceptional growth fast. There are many ways to do this, from investing in new technology, to rapid organic expansion. Another option is to put your money (or the bank's, if you can get it) into acquisitions. All routes carry their own risks.

In fact, hypergrowth should come with a very big government health warning.

Plan it well, or your big drive for hypergrowth could easily destroy everything you have worked so hard to achieve.

My experiment with hypergrowth in 2007 involved recruiting 50 new people in one hit to massively increase the number of policies we wrote. At the time, I already employed 100 people, my business was growing steadily and everything was fine. I was just bored. I wanted to get there quicker.

It immediately became obvious that it was not a strategy for the faint-hearted. On the two open days where we interviewed the candidates, I did experience a sharp intake of breath as I saw this huge crowd of new faces milling around my HQ. These weren't just numbers on my master plan, or 'to do' list; they were real people. Each one of these people, if I took them on, wouldn't only require a decent salary, with all the add-ons that go with it, in terms of national insurance and so on; they'd also require telephones, computers, office space and desks.

But, I went for it.

Did it work? Up to a point. My business certainly grew very rapidly. Indeed, how could we have failed to do so, having expanded my payroll by 50 per cent virtually overnight? Three and a half years down the line, we are undoubtedly still reaping the rewards of this rapid expansion.

But, while it was rapid growth, it wasn't hypergrowth. My mistake, in my eagerness to scale up into hypergrowth, is I didn't prepare enough by scrutinising my systems and internal statistics properly. The exceptional expansion exposed some gaping holes in my business numbers analysis.

Up until that point, I had thought my business' conversion rates stood at 25 per cent. So, for example, if we provided four customers with a quote, one would buy our policy. As it turned out, we were converting more like 18 per cent, but just didn't know it, thanks to a quirk in the back office system. The system was incorrectly exaggerating the conversion rate when one customer bought two policies. So, if someone received a quote for a goods in transit policy and subsequently bought a public liability one too, that would be marked up as converting at 50 per cent. Clearly, this was not the true picture. It is the same customer and in real terms they are only converting at 18 per cent. Some of the business add-ons that we sold as extras, such as a business support pack for just £19, were seriously distorting the figures.

When we were growing organically, this anomaly was not a huge issue. However, once my business was in hypergrowth, where there is far more cash at stake and all the numbers are much bigger, this inaccuracy was leaving me seriously exposed. Having invested all that extra money, I was not making nearly as much income as I had imagined we would make.

As it turned out, this was not the main catalyst which caused me to scale back the hypergrowth strategy after six months. The bulk of my business is with the building and construction industry, which is always the first to suffer in an economic downturn. With the 2008 credit crisis gathering pace, it seemed prudent to halt the hypergrowth for a while.

Sadly, I had to let the 50 extra staff go and continue with my steady-as-she-goes strategy. However, as I said, the brief period of hypergrowth did make a positive and serious long term impact on my business. Even with a slight flaw in my numbers, I could see what could be achieved if you've got the bottle to do it. Fast growth should be the aim of the game for any fortune hunter, although I know there are 'consultants' who would object to that statement. It is the only way to make the progress you need to realise your dreams of making real money.

It is something that I would certainly do again - with a few firm rules in place.

- Big, audacious plan. Be absolutely clear about what it is you want to achieve and why. Achieving hypergrowth is notoriously difficult and if it is not backed by a stable coherent plan, it is virtually impossible. So, if you want to grow to be four times the size in the next 12 months, how are you going to do it?

- Be agile. Hypergrowth, by its very nature, is not a linear path. You need to be aware, opportunistic and nimble on your feet. When something comes along which fits in with the vision, move quickly.

- Scrutinise. Hypergrowth will expose any weaknesses in your core business model. The sums involved are much bigger and the stakes will be higher. It is essential that you know all of your back office systems inside out and backwards, before embarking on a hypergrowth strategy.

- Prepare for known and unknown stumbling blocks. Stay nimble and alert at all times. If something changes the environment you work in, either internally or externally, then be prepared to halt the hypergrowth strategy immediately. I thought I knew my system inside out - and didn't. Then there were the unforeseen events, such as the rapid onset of the recession. I was prepared to react decisively to both.

- Don't let sentiment or pride stand in your way. Business is business. If you have to admit a hypergrowth project ended sooner than you'd like, or to scale back on extra staff, so be it. Learn from it and move on.

Hypergrowth can be done at any time in a business' growth cycle. If you can see that there is a market there for it and you could grow four, six, or even ten times quicker, you would be crazy not to consider it. But plan carefully, because you will put a lot more money at risk and, if you are not very careful, destroy the gains you have already made. Often, once you have put the increase in costs around the plan, it may show you that now is not a good time. That doesn't mean it will never be a good time. Keep it on the agenda and keep doing the sums.

Hypergrowth is not for everyone. It does take a different mindset. You have to be someone who thrives on challenge and change. You also have to be constantly agile and alert. The secret is to stay focused and protect your interests at all times.

Hypergrowth, if you get it right, will lead to hyper-rewards.

Measure, Measure, Measure

Scribble your stuff here

www.diaryofafortunehunter.com
Follow me on twitter@lyndonx

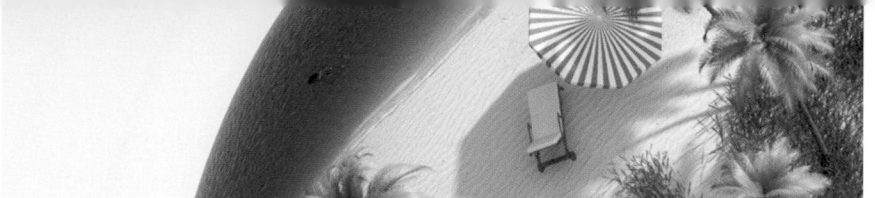

Week 30

Shrink to Grow - Making savings by taking the helicopter view

Every six months or so, I make a point of going abroad to spend some time in a location and atmosphere that is so divorced from my day-to-day business that I could well be on another planet. I don't just do it to take a well-earned break from my corporate endeavours and I certainly don't do it to top up my tan. I do it so that I can step away from everything, take a deep breath and review my business from top to bottom. When I am away, I become my MD's worse nightmare with a bombardment of requests and observations and up to two hour-long daily calls.

This is what lovers of management jargon like to call 'taking a helicopter view' of a business. Yet, just because this relatively simple concept has become a management cliché does not reduce its validity, nor should it put you off. Why not? Well, despite the fact that everyone seems to know what it is that I am doing, very few business owners ever seem to take the time to rise above the detail to see the bigger picture. Some never seem to look up and look around them at all.

All entrepreneurs would benefit from regularly stepping back and engaging their brains to think more clearly about things like structure and future strategy. Yet, there is little point even considering doing this while you are immersed in the thick of running your company. It is almost impossible to look at the bigger picture rationally when you are taken up with the day-to-day grind of the business. But, if you don't look up (or down), a few years down the line you will probably start wondering why you have not fulfilled your ambitions for growth and world domination (if that is what you wanted!).

You have to physically step away in order to get into the right frame of mind.

If you give yourself some distance and height from your business, you'll be able to ask yourself vital questions such as:

- Where is my business going, and is that what I want for both the business and myself?

- What are the opportunities that I can see from my helicopter that I can't usually see from the ground when I am immersed in the business?

- What are the challenges ahead - again, which I can see from my lofty position, but which I may not have previously spotted?

I won't say this is easy. Like any entrepreneur, I loath to leave my business for long. Plus, none of us are born with the natural ability to take the helicopter view. You have to train yourself to do it and it really helps if you physically remove yourself from the business as I do. Some geographic remoteness can work wonders - and it means you can't regularly break off from your strategising to slip back into the office to "check everything is OK".

One of the methods I have used to train myself to look at my business in this way is to ask myself the following question; "How can I shrink to grow?" Now, this may sound like an odd starting point, even a little bit mad, but believe me, it will concentrate your mind in the right direction.

The thinking behind it goes like this: If you come up with ways of shrinking your business in certain areas, you will save money. Cash is, of course, the biggest issue for business owners and most of us have plenty of ideas on how to expand the business, but can't execute them because there is never enough money. Therefore, if you can look at your business in the round to come up with ideas to save money, you will be able to reinvest that money into the business. At the same time, while you are looking at the business in this way, you will also be better placed to identify the best places to invest your cash. Hence, shrink to grow.

By doing this, you will automatically eliminate waste, make plans for the future, identify opportunities and work through any hurdles that might stop you from making things happen.

Areas that generally turn out to be fairly easy to shrink are:

1. Non-sales functions. Do you really need so many admin staff to do tasks such as send faxes, or take messages? There may be simpler and more efficient ways to communicate and investing in new technology, so executives can look after some of their own admin, which could well pay dividends.

2. Non-sales, non-salary costs. Paying out for items such as stationery, utilities and travel can add up to a small fortune. Amazingly, most businesses just seem to accept this and don't ever really scrutinise what they are paying out. If you really put your mind to it, you could make significant savings in this area.

3. Rent. Office space is usually a huge fixed cost for any business. If you are renting, why not see if you can get a reduction from your landlord? You may be pleasantly surprised at the reply and, as the old adage goes, if you don't ask, you won't get.

4. Marketing spend. How much of your marketing activity is actually producing the results you wanted or expected? Give your marketing some careful scrutiny and if you think that it is not working, stop everything now and redistribute the cost saving into a more lucrative part of the business.

I do this exercise regularly, yet I still find significant savings every time. Then, once I have pinpointed how much I can save and from where, I allocate 60 per cent of those savings towards some sort of sales activity. I may use those savings on a piece of marketing that I have identified during my helicopter session, or simply employing more sales executives. The important point is I am regularly making a valuable investment in my business and I have only been able to do this because I have switched from a narrow focus to the big vision. Plus, not only is this profitable for my firm, but it also offers an unlimited source of long term motivation to me on a personal level.

My advice? Develop a great business, then get an airline ticket and don't come back until you've thought of at least half a dozen ways to make it better. Then, repeat this exercise regularly.

Overdeliver

Scribble your stuff here

_____

_____

_____

_____

_____

_____

_____

_____

_____

_____

_____

Week 31

Evolve or Die - Taking the next big leap by thinking in a new way

Have you ever wondered why that best friend of yours moved on from you and become a hugely successful multi-millionaire? Or maybe how some people seem to come from nowhere and become the CEO of an incredibly successful global firm?

It is because they *evolve*.

These people are, quite simply, different from ordinary folk. They see things in different ways. They never let the dust settle under their feet or stand still. They are always looking to learn and grow their knowledge across all sorts of sectors, regardless if it has got anything to do with what they are doing right now.

They basically never stop asking questions and weighing up what things mean to them. EVER.

Over the years I have met many enormously successful business people from Steve Ridgway, the CEO of Virgin Atlantic, to Stelios Haji-Ioannou, the easyJet founder, to hotel entrepreneur Rocco Forte, and they all have these characteristics in common. What is perhaps most striking, is they all have knowledge way beyond the scope of their core businesses and an intellectual curiosity to constantly learn even more. You cannot help but surmise that if you want to build a multi-million pound empire you cannot do so by being insular. You have to be constantly aware of what is going on around you in your business, the economy and the world. You have to keep asking questions and then relate the information back to your core business to make better, more impactful, decisions.

The alternative? Get stale, wither and die.

The truth of this was really brought home to me in the early days of the credit crunch. The moment I saw the global economy begin to turn in 2007, I started looking hard at my industry and in particular, my own company. Nearly two thirds of my insurance business is concerned with the construction sector, and knowing that this industry is always the first to suffer in a downturn, I immediately took steps to brace my firm for the anticipated dip in sales.

If I had not prepared myself, I could easily have been plunged into a complete disaster. Strangely enough, what happened next was a complete surprise. My sales actually soared! Again, instead of sitting back and counting my good fortune that I had survived, I looked carefully into the phenomenon and how I might exploit it. It turned out that many builders were setting themselves up in business, having been laid off by the big boys in the recession. I was therefore getting a raft of new enquiries from this enterprising new sector. This insight gave me the opportunity to immediately focus a section of my business towards serving this new breed of builder.

To be a successful fortune hunter, you have to be constantly alert and willing to evolve just like this. For some people, this may mean completely changing your mindset, away from the ordinary and into seeing the extraordinary. It may even mean learning to think in an entirely new way.

If you are not lucky enough to naturally have this drive, curiosity and persistence, now is the time to upgrade your brain so it is geared towards seeking out new knowledge and opportunity at every turn.

Here's how:

1. *Forget the ego.* Most normal people make protecting their ego a priority, particularly if they are in a position where they want to be seen as a success. If they don't understand something, or are not sure they have the full picture, they'll keep schtum. They don't want to lose face by asking awkward questions. A true fortune hunter, on the other hand, will subject all and sundry with a barrage of questions until they find out what they need to know. They don't care what other people think. They know that knowledge is power and won't stop until they have the full picture. (This also explains why fortune hunters have to run their own show - they'd drive their bosses mad with their incessant questioning if they were an ordinary employee!)

2. *Think big.* Ordinary people look at an exciting new product and think, "Wow, how do I get one of those?" What does a fortune hunter think? They are busy working out how they can produce one (or something similar) for their own industry and make it even better.

3. *Be positive.* The normal human reaction to a challenging idea is to explore all the reasons why it may not work and what might go wrong. Such negativity doesn't distract a true fortune hunter. They don't give headroom to all the potential downsides until they have a clear vision as to how the concept might succeed. Then, if it looks like a goer, they give it a try.

4. *Be restless.* Change terrifies most people. Indeed, most ordinary business owners thank their lucky stars when things are rumbling on OK and do their utmost to keep everything the same. The status quo bores fortune hunters. They are always looking to make things (even good things) better even if it does cause a little disruption. And, just as I did in the credit crunch, they are constantly on the look out for new threats or opportunities.

5. *Don't dream.* Forget daydreaming of making piles of cash - that is for schoolkids. Analyse what has worked and what hasn't in your firm and in others, and then make your ambitions a reality by putting your plans into action.

These qualities are what differentiate fortune hunters from the rest of the world. They ask questions and get on with it, while others are looking the other way, or worse still, not looking at all.

The aim of the game is to evolve and keep evolving if you want to make a mark and show real progress. Get started by asking some questions. Then, don't stop.

"To ask is but a moment's shame, not to ask and remain ignorant is a lifelong shame."

Summary

Great businesses become great businesses because they are continually driven from the top. Fortune hunters don't accept mediocre – they are always looking for the best. You must be constantly on the lookout for the best people and then drive and motivate them to do even better. Similarly, your company will only thrive if you constantly tell everyone about how good it is and then keep on telling them. None of this means that you should not keep an eye on costs, because if you let them run away with you, you will erode all your good work in a heartbeat. Get it right and you will be well on the way.

AUTUMN

Just because you have started your business and it is ticking along nicely, it does not mean that it will ever remain like this.

Situations will arise every day that will bite you on the backside if you are not vigilant and constantly on the lookout for problems. Besides which, you are never going to make it as a fortune hunter if you are prepared to sit back and tick along. The Autumn troubleshooting section highlights some of the things that can go wrong and what to do about it.

Don't think, ACT.

Scribble your stuff here

Week 32

Know All or Complacent?

One of the biggest news stories for a decade must surely be the hacking scandal which has dogged Rupert Murdoch and his News Corp empire. For a while, every new day brought out a fresh angle on the tale. Meanwhile, a succession of senior managers stepped up to say they had no idea what was really going on in the highly successful firm.

It got me thinking. Were Rupert Murdoch and his trusted lieutenants being complacent in the way they ran their empire? Did they look the other way to concentrate on the 'bigger picture', while those lower down the ranks interpreted what they thought needed to be done?

It will take many months, probably even years, to get to the bottom of it and I would not presume to judge the outcome of those high level investigations. My personal view is they were not complacent. In any organisation, large or small, it does not matter how many reporting procedures you put in down the line, it is virtually impossible to completely cover the day-to-day actions of your employees. Things do slip through. In News Corp's case, it just happened that what slipped through was something which had major long term repercussions.

None of this means that you can shrug your shoulders and say what will be, will be. To begin with the premise that you're probably going to miss something, so you may as well relax, would be a very dangerous strategy. This sort of complacency kills businesses. Indeed, I strongly believe that complacency is a major contributing factor to why many companies fail. You don't often read about it in business articles, but the truth is, too many firms are passively accepting of 'OK' results, or late reporting of figures by the team, or missed challenges, or things that are just not quite good enough. Yet, so many of these things pave the way to the business graveyard.

So, how do you avoid complacency in your business? Canny fortune hunters should be constantly focusing their attention and energy on three areas:

People

There is an old saying; 'the system is only as good as the people who execute it'. That saying is as true today as it ever was. The first, and arguably most important, anti-complacency step has to be to regularly assess everyone who works for and around you. You have to know what they are doing, how they are doing it and what they may be missing.

Proper reporting is key. To give you an idea, the type of regular reports I insist on in my business are:

- Daily sales accounts. These numbers are automatically generated and sent to me via email, every single day.

- Compliance report. This weekly report immediately highlights any system breaches or issues.

- Management accounts. These accounts that analyse the previous month's trading are produced, without fail, on the 7th of each month.

- Monthly information pack. This document provides me with details of the income for each product line, together with customer conversion rates by source. We even throw in some nice graphs as an instant and highly visual reckoner of growth or shrinkage.

I'm not just generating paperwork, or email traffic either. I study each of these documents in minute detail and act on anything that concerns me. I rely on them to tell me everything I need to know and would be lost without them.

I also hold a weekly briefing with all of my co-directors to go through any current risks and challenges. I am constantly looking to identify what might need to change, by when and am always mindful of the consequences of not responding when the need clearly arises.

Plus, don't forget that one of the most useful things you can do is simply walk around your business and speak with the staff on the front line. Ask how are they getting on and how do they do what they do and funnily enough, they'll probably tell you.

Plans

Planning should not be something you do, then simply get on with making it happen. It's a good start, but not the be all and end all. Planning is not a static event. Things in business change. All the time. (If they don't, you ain't doing it right)

If you want to avoid the complacency trap, you should adopt a dynamic process of constantly challenging assumptions, testing the market and following up any changes that have affected your original plan. You should be prepared to commit generous amounts of time to this continuous adjustment, which means constantly being on guard for anything which distracts you from this task (see 'Week 44, Control your randoms - Ignore distractions').

Make sure you are continuously asking and answering these questions:

- Where are we now?

- Where do we want to be?

- How will we get there?

- How are we doing?

Address these questions all the time and think about them in terms of your employees and directors too. If you question thoroughly, listen to the responses carefully and take action when needed, you won't become complacent.

Process

I've talked a lot about the importance of process elsewhere, but its role in anti-complacency cannot be underestimated and therefore it deserves a staring role here too.

You should be regularly reviewing the essential processes that produce results for your business, be it technology, sales, marketing, operations or financial. Similarly, you should constantly be asking yourself if there are any other areas where you are putting up with waste, either in time or money. Once you've identified all of these critical areas, then sketch out a flow chart of each step in that process.

- Are you satisfied with the efficiency and effectiveness of each step?

- Are the right people running this process?

- Do you have ideas on how to improve the process by 10 per cent or better?

Even if you do this pretty regularly, you'll be amazed at the complacency that can creep into your critical processes over time.

The thing to remember about complacency is, even if you are on the right track, you will get run over if you just sit there.

Yes, it is impossible to have systems and controls in place to take into account every single day-to-day action of each and every employee, but if you've got both eyes wide open and you've got proper reporting structures in place, you won't miss much. You'll certainly be better off than those folks who are always just too busy to look at their business properly and then wonder why it all goes up in smoke.

Actions speak louder than words but that depends who is talking

Scribble your stuff here

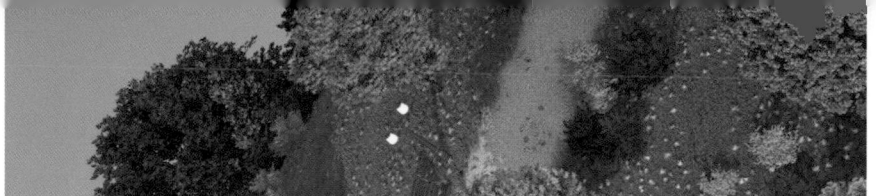

Week 33

Seven Deadly Blockers - Why firms fail

Beware of the business blocker! We all have them. Everything is rumbling along at a steady pace and, all of a sudden, it hit the hurdle and grinds to a halt. All your big moneymaking plans suddenly don't seem so easy.

Over the years, I have encountered a lot of blockers. Do you know what I have discovered? They fall into seven broad categories and once you know what they are, it is actually pretty easy to find a way through them.

Some of these blockers - and how to guard against them - are covered in more detail elsewhere in the diary. However, it's great to have a quick and ready checklist to see why things are not going as planned to help you cut through the proverbial as and when it strikes.

So, here goes with my seven business blockers:

1. Cash

Cash has to be number one on the list. Over a third of small and medium sized businesses suffer cash flow problems so severe that the business itself is threatened. There can be a variety of reasons, but the most common are late payments, slow product or service turnaround times, failure to perform new client credit checks or a sudden change in the market. There are dozens more reasons besides.

The point to remember is; cash is always the biggest restriction in business. If you understand and accept that, then you are halfway there.

You need to plan ahead, guard against the reasons above and identify when you may need to get in some extra cash to see you through. Options of how you may access that cash (in ascending order of recommendation, with the best sources first) include:

- Drawings from profits - assuming there are some.

- Remortgaging your home. Assuming you have equity in your property, this can often be the most cost-effective way to raise capital.

- Raising capital from a private investor. This can be a great option if that investor is able to add value to the business in other ways.

- Bank loan or overdraft. This is difficult in today's market, so it is best not to rely on this as a source.

- Grants. Good luck with this one. The government have really tightened up in this area, so it is not an easy option either.

- Loan from a family member. On the plus side, this will make you look very carefully at your business plan. However, any business dealings with family should carry a large government health warning. (See 'Week 13: Don't keep things in the family - ever!')

- Credit cards, although this should be a last resort because of the crippling rates of interest.

Finally, as a short term measure, don't forget to look at ways of reducing costs in your business by reviewing your processes. (see 'Week 50: Squeeze the Juice').

2. No space to strategise.

When you are running a business day in and day out, there is a natural tendency to get so bogged down in the detail that it starts to become impossible to think strategically about the business, its future and any growth potential. It is even possible to forget about this side of things altogether, which is hardly a good sign for a would-be fortune hunter. I recommend you regularly review what takes up most of your time and make a judgement about whether it really needs to be you doing it. It's fair enough that you empty the wastepaper bins when you are a one-man band, but if you are still doing it when the company is 20 people strong, you have seriously strayed down the wrong path.

It may be that you need to employ a really hands-on manager to take on all these tasks so you can release your time to think of growth opportunities and, more importantly, execute them. If you cannot afford full time wages, consider bringing in a retired person for just two days a week. Believe me, this will take the brakes off any business and will transform your company.

3. Ignorance

If you come up against a brick wall, or something that is seriously hampering your growth, don't just sit there - do something! I am amazed when people tell me that they are having sleepless nights over some problem, yet seem unable or unwilling to do something about it.

I have always acknowledged my weaknesses (yes, I do have some!) and pride myself on the fact that if I do not know something, I will go and find out how to do it. Straight away. It doesn't matter if it is a problem to do with the economy, an industry sector, a stock management issue, or some torturous financial instrument I can't get to grips with.

Knowledge is your greatest asset. If you don't know it, you can't apply it.

4. Technology

This point is related to the above, but worth breaking out, because technology is often one of the major business blockers. A good example from my neck of the woods was the amount of time (and, therefore, my money) my call centre staff were wasting at one stage. Historically, the staff would call up a number on their screen and then hang up if they got a dead dialling tone or answering machine. Then they would laboriously repeat the exercise again. One day I did a calculation and discovered that up to 65 per cent of their time was being wasted on this repetitive activity which had no chance of generating any revenue. So, I looked into my options and invested in an automatic dialler, which eliminates dead tones and answering machines. It cost me tens of thousands of pounds, but the return on investment (ROI) was exceptional.

5. Process

Just because something has always been done in one way doesn't mean that it is always the best way to do it. As a business grows, things change and so should you. It is with this in mind that I watch processes in my company like a hawk.

A case in point would be the use of a fax machine (yes, some companies still have them). If staff have to cross the room, or go to a different floor to send a fax, guess what? It'll invariably take 15 minutes longer than needed because they'll stop to gossip with colleagues along the way, nip to the toilet, or use it as an excuse for a cigarette break. All of this is costing you money and there are numerous examples of this in every company, adding up to thousands of wasted minutes. Look at your processes and make sure you utilise all the up-to-date technology at your fingertips to stamp out the time-wasting. In the case of the fax, for example, it is easy to install software into PCs at almost zero cost so they can send faxes straight from their desk. If you spot other process blockers, find a way to bring them up-to-date.

6. Businesses outgrow staff

It's true. You will outgrow some, if not all, your early employees. People become attached to a small business set-up. When there are, say, only a dozen or so people in the company, staff welcome the fact that they can cross the floor and have a chat with the boss. Then, as your business grows, some people will feel that they have been increasingly cut off from the centre of power. Do you know what they do then? They become business blockers. They try to hold the business back so it can be like it was in the old days. You'll alter a process so you can grow, and they will quietly change it back to the old way.

Not everyone is like this. Some people will evolve and rise to the challenge. But many people will get left behind. It sounds brutal, but you have to deal with this, or they will continue to hold you back, either overtly or covertly. You can try to help them change their ways, but if they are utterly intransigent, then you may consider it is time for a parting of the ways.

7. Failure to adapt

I am a great believer in specialisation, as are many businesses, but don't be so wedded to 'doing what you do' that you ignore all the warning signs that things are awry in your sector. While it is great to be known for a particular product, service or price point, it can become restrictive when the market changes and you trudge on regardless. All of sudden your single-mindedness will leave you with yesterday's trend, or stock at a price which is vastly different from the new kid on the street. Keep your eyes open and your mind sharp.

Keep all of the above blockers constantly in mind, guard against them and you will soon experience exponential and profitable growth.

"And that's the boss. Nice enough guy, but wood from the neck up, if you know what I mean!"

> *If you are in business, then be in business,*
> *don't play at it.*

Scribble your stuff here

Week 34

Be a Sniper - The efficient way to solve problems!

People often ask me what I do for a living. My usual reply is, "I am a sales person", because as a business owner that is what you are. You are selling to everyone, all the time, whether it is a new customer, an investor, the media, or a supplier. If, however, I am feeling mischievous, I might say to my inquisitor, "I am a sniper". Most people will be utterly bewildered by this answer and I am sure you are also now wondering what exotic substance I might be on today.

Let me explain. All businesses have challenges and challenges are, as we all know, a euphemism for cock-ups, problems, and complete clangers. As a business owner, it is your job to permanently have your sights primed to find out what these issues are.

Then, once you spot a blunder, you need to evaluate it and compare it to the other 'challenges' in the business. Once you've done this, you can pick out a worthy target by prioritising the biggest threat, estimate the scale of that threat and then eliminate it with the minimum of fuss. See, just like a sniper.

Joking aside, this is a very important point. Even if you have managed to gather around you the most dedicated, loyal and active team of staff, they will never see issues in the same way that you, as the business owner, will. They have different priorities and will more naturally focus on their day-to-day tasks. Indeed, it is often not possible to spot looming problems when you are stuck into the nitty-gritty, but if the head of the business is taking the helicopter view (see 'Week 30: Shrink to Grow - Making savings by taking the helicopter view') they should be more than aware of them. Then, they have just got to be dealt with appropriately.

So, how does being a business sniper work? You (and your staff) will probably be relieved to hear there are no guns or telescopic sights involved, just a series of pretty straightforward short steps to follow. Like so many things in running a business, a lot of it is sheer common sense. The five steps to efficient problem solving are:

1. **Identify the problem.** Businesses suffer all the time from a variety of small problems, hiccups, setbacks and stuff just not going quite how you'd like it. The trick is to identify the big, business-threatening, problems which need eliminating or solving with great haste. That means having a thorough understanding of the short and long term implications of each possible threat and some skills at sifting the irrelevant from the relevant so you don't overreact to every small obstacle.

2. **Open-mindedness.** Although a true sniper needs to work fast before their target shifts and the moment is lost, being too hasty as a business sniper can have disastrous consequences. Once you think you know what the problem is, take a deep breath and go through all the information available again. If you approach any problem with a closed mind and think you already know it all, you will slip up and could make a terrible mistake. After all, it might just be that the problem may not be a problem at all, it could be an opportunity.

3. **Look at the cause.** While you are taking your breather, look at the root of this problem. If you eliminate it, is it likely to reoccur? Be careful to ask yourself whether you are simply tackling the symptoms and not the core cause of the issue. You don't want to keep returning to it.

4. **Devise a simple solution.** Think of all the ways you might solve the problem and then go for the simplest, most doable, solution. Don't tie yourself in knots with complex and costly ideas. There is always an easier way.

5. **Do it!** Don't spend days discussing and pontificating. Once you have settled on an appropriate course of action, set a deadline and get it sorted. Remember too, it is not your sole responsibility to carry out the solution. You can delegate it to your team and let them put things right. It might even help stop things going awry again.

How does this work in practice? A recent example for me was a project I started a little while back. I had charged a hand-picked team with setting up a small offshoot venture, which would be complimentary to my main insurance business. I had clearly set out the aims of this new business, what I wanted it to achieve and how I thought they should go about achieving it. A month or so passed and I saw no sign at all of any progress in setting up this subsidiary. There was no launch date set and no clear business plan. In fact, I seemed to be spending a lot of money for not very much return. Naturally, I became rather unnerved by this and called the team in. I had to take control of the situation.

During the meeting, I kept an open mind and listened to what had been going on to date. I asked numerous questions about the market, the issues they had been having and where any difficulties were arising. By doing this and listening carefully, I was immediately able to spot a weak spot in their plan. I offered them a quick and easy solution around the problem and told them to go away, resolve it and move the project up a gear. They did and I am pleased to say this subsidiary is now up and running successfully.

It should go without saying that, if you are running a company, you should make it your business to know what is going on in every area. If you are doing this, you will easily be able to spot any weaknesses, make them your priority and find a quick and easy solution.

Be a sniper, pick your target and fire your bullets.

"Apparently many companies experience problems including: a lack of direction, poor accountability, lack of respect among members, pushing personal agendas, poor communication ..."

Scribble your stuff here

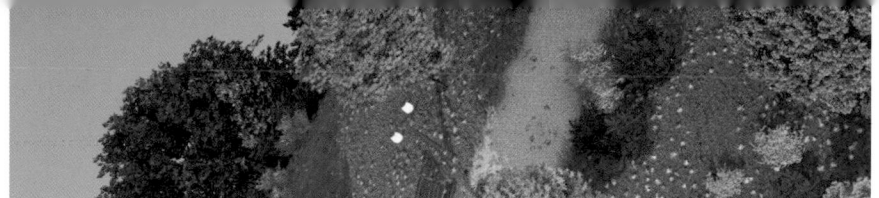

Week 35

Go looking for trouble - Staying motivated

Fortune hunters take a path that not many people are willing to travel down. They take more risks than nine till fivers and can see value and visions where others see nothing. They also probably tackle more challenges before breakfast, than most paid workers attempt in a month.

Obviously, if they get it right, the rewards are substantial and well beyond anything they might earn in an 'ordinary' paid job. But it's not easy. In fact, sometimes it can be pretty tough, frustrating and downright exhausting.

The question that I often get asked by people just starting out on their entrepreneurial adventure is, "How do you stay motivated?" Yes, it's fine when everything is going great, they say, but on the days when things seem to be crashing down around their ears, it's pretty hard to go on smiling.

My initial reaction to this question is that I'm pretty lucky in that I have always lived and breathed business, which means lack of drive has never been a big threat. I have an inbuilt, natural motivation and a burning desire to prove the naysayers wrong. I never imagine for a moment that anything can beat me (how could it?) and any sign of defeatism in others drives me mad. In fact, the tougher the challenge, the better I perform.

But, there is more to staying motivated than this. Thinking more deeply about it, I realised that I have also zealously guarded against anything that may sap my get-up-and-go. How do I do it? By constantly looking for trouble.

People suffer from lack of motivation because they get to a good place, like what they are doing and then take their foot off the gas. In short, they get complacent. Their bills are getting paid, everyone is congratulating them for running a steady ship and they may even have managed to put aside a little bit of cash for a rainy day. Without realising it, they'd have settled.

What do you think will happen next? Yup, they'll be bored out of their tiny minds. All that entrepreneurial drive, the ambition, the constant stream of ideas, will still be in there, but will have no outlet. The result? Lack of motivation, frustration and misery.

The best way to guard against this downward spiral is to constantly go looking for trouble. I never stop seeking out challenges in the business, such as systems that might go wrong, or products that have gone off the boil, or shifts in the industry. Then I sort them out. (See 'Week 34: Be a Sniper - The efficient way to solve problems!' for some tips on how to do this)

Of course, this means my team often say to me, "You are always complaining about problems and looking for the worse case scenario. Why don't you give us a pat on the back instead?" I always reply that it is my job to find the issues and add value to the business. If I constantly dished out praise, they'd get complacent and lose their drive. It is only by keeping an ever watchful eye out for trouble that we will grow and improve. That's my job.

Plus, because I am always in the thick of the action, I am constantly motivated and excited about my company.

Even so, I do accept that there will always be bad days. Maybe you won't get a contract you really worked hard for. Perhaps one of your respected senior colleagues who you really rely upon decides to go elsewhere. Or someone you had previously thought really highly of drops a real (and business-damaging) clanger. Or a competitor pulls a fast one.

It is with this in mind that I have some suggestions for quick motivational fixes to get you looking on the bright side again. Some may work for you and some might not. Try them all and see which ones get you smiling again:

- *Read inspirational books.* Like this one! Seriously, it is good to hear about how other people have got through the trials of scaling up their own business.

- *Read entrepreneurial blogs.* They are a great way to get a daily update on what other business owners are up to and how they overcome various hiccups. Twitter and LinkedIn are also great resources.

- *Make friends with fellow entrepreneurs.* There is nothing better than a face-to-face chat with people like you to realise that these ups and downs are perfectly normal. Make a point of getting out to meet fellow entrepreneurs. Before you know it, you'll be sharing a coffee and laughing about a problem that a few weeks back got you close to throwing in the towel.

- *Surround yourself with positive people.* Following on from the above, make sure your confidants are positive thinkers. There is nothing more mind-numbingly destructive than talking to people who always see the worst in everything. Ditch the naysayers. Now.

- *Passion and strength from within.* Remind yourself why you are doing what you are doing. You probably started your business because you always wanted to run your own show. You may well have previously been in a job you hated. Or it may have been that your idea for a company was just so overwhelmingly right that you knew you had to do it. Or, it could have been all of the above. All you need to do is remember that sense of pride and ambition you felt on the first day you started trading as My Great Company Ltd.

- *Look for small measures of success.* OK, you missed out on that contract, or really screwed up that deal. But what have you done right? Give yourself a mental pat on the back for the small triumphs (and big ones) that are all part of making good progress to your final goal.

- *Visualise the end results.* Some fortune hunters swear by visualisation techniques and literally put a picture of what they are working for in a place they can regularly see it. If a screen saver of a 16-bedroomed mansion, or a framed picture of a Ferrari F50, gives you a boost, don't be shy.

The best motivator by far for a fortune hunter is to think about the unlimited possibilities in front of them. If you made £1,000 on that bit of the business today, you could make £10,000 next time, then £100,000, then £1 million. There is absolutely nothing to stop you except for yourself. What are you waiting for? And remember, no matter what the issues are, they are just growing pains.

There is always a way

Scribble your stuff here

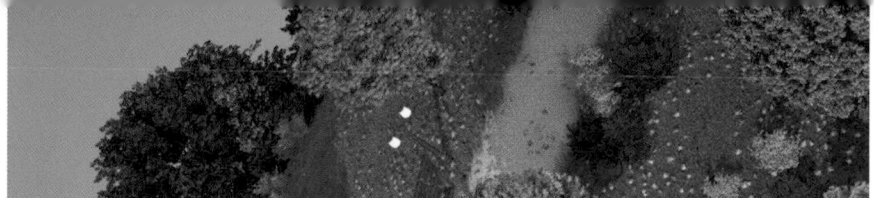

Week 36

Think like a start-up -
Keep your business fresh

Why is it that the most innovative breakthroughs come from new businesses? You know the sort of thing. A company which apparently comes from nowhere is run on a shoestring, with practically no resources and no preconceptions about how things are 'done' in the real world. Then, overnight, suddenly everyone is talking about this company and the big boys are left scrabbling in its wake, desperate to get a piece of the action.

Start-ups can do this because they have no 'baggage'. They are not too busy doing-it-this-way-because-that's-what-we've-always-done. They are not restricted by cares over killing the golden goose if they introduce something a bit different into the main business. They don't think it is better to give a micro improvement a go in case it doesn't all work out.

Quite simply, start-ups look at the world in a different way.

Which got me thinking. Would it be possible for me to look at my business as a start-up, even though it has been around for over two decades?

To put this to the test, I decided to tackle a problem that had been bugging me for eight months or more, but which I really had no clue how to solve. The issue I had grappled with was how to deal with one of my distribution channels, which wasn't performing nearly as well as any of my other three distribution channels.

I asked myself, "What if that underperforming channel was my only distribution channel (or even business) and the other three never existed? Plus, what if this channel was a start-up operation?" Suddenly, the mists lifted. Thinking like this was a complete revelation.

I realised that what I had done is built on a complex, one-size-fits-all, infrastructure for my whole business. Beginning with the idea that I wanted to significantly scale up the company, I had dragged every part of the business along, regardless of the fact that some bits were not suited to this structure.

At a glance, I could see that I did not need so many people in this badly performing channel and that many of the job functions I did have could be easily shared with my other divisions. If that was my only business, I simply did not need that infrastructure or all those people servicing it. I had been swept away by my ambitions for the whole business, at the expense of thinking what each part of the business really needed.

By going right back to basics, I could completely transform the fortunes of this part of the business by paring it back and then giving it the right fuel it needed to grow.

After this exercise, I was inspired by the start-up mindset and started thinking how I could apply it to other areas of my business. To do this, I set out the core philosophies that make start-ups different.

They are:

- Speed. Ignore the tortoise and hare story. That is just kid's stuff. No, if you want to get on in business, fast beats slow, or speed beats perfection. Every time. Even my number plate reads 2 SLO, I believe that much. Start-ups are fleet of foot and use their speed to their advantage. They are halfway to the finish line while most big companies are discussing policy, or where to have the annual away day.

- Curiosity. People behind start-ups are curious. They are constantly asking, "What if? Why? Wouldn't this be better?" They are not weighed down by colleagues shaking their heads and saying, "Well, we tried that in 1999 and it didn't work then." No, start-ups know there must be a better way and are prepared to try something. Even if some smart alec says it didn't quite work before.

- Disregard for the status quo. Do you remember that feeling of you against the world? It's great, isn't it? Nothing fires you up more than the desire to put two fingers up to the complacent market leaders, or the people who told you it can't be done. Imagine what could happen if you could hold on to that energy? Always.

- Feel no fear. It takes balls to start a business. There are many unknowns and the price of failure could be catastrophic. People who begin businesses learn how to conquer that fear. Unfortunately, as time goes on, many business owners are not quite so keen to risk everything to move forward.

No matter what business you are in, thinking like a start-up will add a whole new angle to your business and could seriously refresh any jaded areas. What is more, it could transform the way you view and interact with your company.

I am constantly amazed by how many once brave entrepreneurs gradually slip into an employment mentality. From setting out as a gutsy start-up, with lots of great ideas, they slowly relax, settle down and behave pretty much the same as they did when they had a job in their previous lives. Suddenly, they'll be insisting on five weeks off a year and will tell clients that they "don't work weekends". I even know some businesses that still close on a Wednesday - madness! Their smartphones will be switched off at 5.30pm sharp and emails will go unanswered until 'reasonable' business hours.

Then, they will bemoan the fact that their business is not as big as they hoped it might be, or the profit seems to be levelling off.

Here is a news flash for people like that, in case they have forgotten what it is like to be in a start-up: if you want to succeed in business and make your fortune; it is a 24-7 occupation. You will never switch off - either your smartphone, or your brain. It is like this from the moment you begin the venture, until it becomes a multi-million pound organisation and beyond. The demands of the business will always be onerous and if you want to be a success, you've got to put the time, energy and emotional commitment into it.

If you don't like the sound of that, stop reading now. Get a job and good luck to you.

All businesses, whether large or small, old or young, would benefit from regularly reviewing things from a start-up point of view. Pinpoint problem areas and work through them as though you were just setting up the company and this is one of the hurdles to getting it off the ground. I guarantee you will see your business in a different light and will start seeing a whole pool of people and processes you just don't need.

It is all to do with getting the right frame of mind. But, if you can capture just a fraction of that conquer-the-world start-up feeling, you will be amazed at what you can achieve.

Never take "can't be done" as an answer to an issue

Scribble your stuff here

Week 37

Hit the refresh button -
Ways to give your business a boost

Let's face it, all businesses slow down now and again. Most entrepreneurs don't like admitting it, because it doesn't fit in with the gung-ho persona of a business leader sweating over challenges long into the night, day after day and year after year. But, if we are honest, all of us quite frequently find ourselves coasting along in neutral, wondering where to go next. I know I have and I don't mind admitting it. As soon as I see this happening though, I always hit the refresh button to re-energise the business and get it motoring once again.

The alternative, if you let the business stutter along for too long a period, is that it could stall altogether and be impossible to restart.

"Enough with the motoring analogies Lyndon," you may be thinking. "What do you mean by hitting the refresh button?"

Well, trial and error have shown me that there are a number of ways to get things fizzing again. These are:

- Reinvent. Similarly to the idea of thinking like a start-up in last week's entry, imagine you had just bought your business. What would you do? The normal chain of events for a new owner is to review every aspect of the firm, from personnel to systems, from products to client relationships. If you were looking at this company with a fresh pair of eyes and wanted to make more money, would you change anything? Or I should say: What would you change?

- Micro-segment. There is always something good in your business that you have never spotted before. Breakdown all the areas you operate in and give yourself an honest evaluation of how each one is doing. If you are honest, really honest, areas where you are really flying will emerge. At the same time, those areas where you are limping along will be painfully apparent too. However, if you segment down those painful areas even further, there could be a hidden gem there too. You know what to do next.

- Follow-up on old/lapsed customers. Very often, in the race to grow, we put all our energies into snapping up as many new customers as possible. That's great, but are you forgetting about your old or lapsed customers? Loyal customers are the lifeblood of your business and if someone has worked with you once and moved on, they may be more inclined to come back with a bit of persuasion. It is certainly dangerous to assume that a lapsed customer will never buy from you again. Take a bit of time out to get in touch with your customer base and find out what needs they have, or to remind them of what a great service you offer. Make the effort to make contact because it will pay dividends.

- Cross-sell. Are your clients aware of everything you do? Don't assume they are, because they probably are not. Start thinking of an innovative way to introduce them to other parts of your business.

- Stop giving parts of your business away. In any business, there are bits that you let other people do because you think they will be better at it. But are they? In my line of work, we gather an awful lot of data in our day-to-day business. In the past, we have sold this on. One day, I got to thinking that maybe we could do something with it and, once we started really wringing the data we had, we created all sorts of other business opportunities. I couldn't believe we hadn't thought of it before.

- Ditch the energy vampires. Are there certain members of the team that are sapping your energy and verve? Very often, when you have these stagnant periods, it is because all your efforts are being diverted into helping the needs of one or two difficult members of the team. Some people do have the ability to suck all the life out of all those around them, even the most dedicated and determined of entrepreneurs. It may well be time to tell the energy vampires to get off the bus and do one.

- Smile. Yes, it is corny, but it is so true. If the business leader looks slumped, demotivated and, well, bored, how do you think the team is going to feel? You set the tone for how your team respond to every situation. Plus, once you make an effort to smile, you'd be amazed how much better you'll feel.

Most importantly, you have to ACT. There is no point assessing the problems, thinking about new ways forward and mentally listing the barriers in your way. Work out what is wrong and then get on with putting things right. If you spend days or weeks pontificating, dozens of opportunities will have passed you by. That doesn't mean you have to be rash, and rush from one new idea to another. Just find a balance. Think it through, weigh it up and get on with it.

One of the most important things not to do when day-to-day business seems to be becoming mundane is to overreact and rush off to diversify into new areas.

Stick to your knitting! While it is always good to look at more ways to make money, don't even consider diversifying until you have maximised ALL the opportunities in your own, existing market (see 'Week 28: Diversify or not? Great ideas to expand your business with minimal risk', for more details on this). It is too easy (particularly when you feel in a slump) to think the grass may be greener elsewhere and to divert valuable resources, teams and energy into a completely different industry. It won't be greener though. By setting up a completely new venture, all you will be doing is diluting and damaging your core business and setting yourself up for a big fall in an area you don't really know an awful lot about.

I have fallen into the trap of diversifying before I need to, to fill my entrepreneurial hunger. Most of these diversified businesses have done OK. But, if I am honest, if I had stuck with the core strategy in my original firm and devoted all my energies into that, I would have got on at least twice as fast. It is a salient lesson.

So, when you feel in a slump, look at your core business model and work out what you could do better. In fact, even if you are not slowing down, it is a good idea to hit the refresh button at least once a year and work through the list above. Chances are you'll be able to give dozens of areas of your company a whole new lease of life.

Refreshing a business is all about figuring out why you are not making the money you think you should be making, and then doing something about it. So, go hit the refresh button in your firm.

Scribble your stuff here

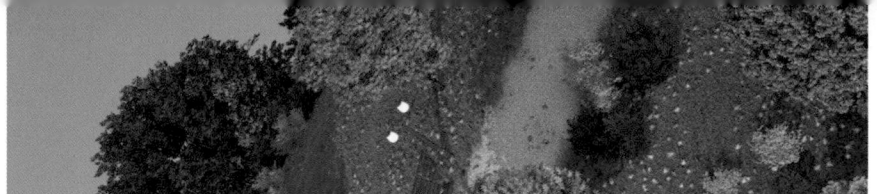

Week 38

Rewire It - What to do when things go (very) wrong

It doesn't matter how good you are, how original your ideas, or how uncluttered your market; sooner or later things will go wrong. What you need to decide is whether it is a slight hiccup in the path towards your big payday, or if it is something which could have a serious, possibly disastrous, impact.

First things first. Stop. Take a deep breath. Don't panic. Take three steps back and take the time to consider what is really going on here. Which of the two camps does your bad day fit into? Is it a minor niggle, or a major stumbling block?

In the case of the former, things often just look a lot worse than they are. There is so much 'noise' in a business with staff issues, sales blips, competitive pressure and so on, that it is often hard to see through it all. That is why stepping back and looking at it in a calm manner is so useful. It may even help to get a big piece of paper, sketch out all the elements which seem so insurmountable and look deep into the numbers, to realise that it is not such a big deal after all.

If this is the case, it may be that you just need to Hit the Refresh Button (see 'Week 37 - Hit the refresh buton - Ways to give your business a boost').

If, however, the problems seem deeper set and have long term implications, you may need to rewire your business. What do I mean by this? I mean get rid of all the things that are dragging you down. It doesn't matter if it is people, a process, or even an entire department. It is time to get in there and get your hands dirty.

While all businesses are different, in my experience, major, business-threatening, problems usually fall into one or more of eight camps. Therefore, you may well find my 'rewiring' checklist a useful guide to get you started on addressing the most common mistakes.

In no particular order, those prime mistakes (and the first steps to remedying them) are:

1.   Complacency. Business doesn't just happen. All too often entrepreneurs forget all the hard-learned lessons of the early days and take their foot off the pedal once things look good. Guess what? The business will gradually grind to a halt and if

you leave it too long, it'll be pretty tough to restart. Get off your backside and get motivated. Make those calls, go and see people and give your team a rocket. You really don't have a moment to lose.

2. Bad credit control. We all know that lack of finance is the biggest killer of start-ups, because if you don't have enough money, you won't be able to do all the things you want to do, or take advantage of any of the opportunities offered to you. So don't get into this position. If your cash flow is rocky, payments are delayed, your credit checks are woeful and late payments are the norm, you are going to be in for a world of hurt if you don't sort it out straightaway. Consider getting in a financial heavyweight to give your accounts department the shake-up it so clearly needs. Plus, if you plan ahead (see point 4) you won't end up borrowing too much money externally and paying crippling interest repayment charges.

3. Misplaced priorities. In the rush to build the infrastructure around your business, get a great office, add on staff numbers and show what a success you are, did you forget the number one reason you are here? Your business will only survive (let alone thrive) if you continuously work on building sales and driving performance. Rethink your sales strategy. Now. Plus, while you are realigning your priorities, give some thought to what actually makes you profit. Quite often, it will be those bits of the business that don't seem all that exciting because you've been doing them a while, but now is the time to rekindle your interest in what really counts.

4. Bad planning. Do you remember that business plan you wrote for your bank, back in the beginning? You did it for a reason and that reason wasn't just to secure a small overdraft. It was a guide to where you were going and how you intended to get there. All businesses need to write regular

plans for at least the next 12 months and then to follow these plans. If you don't, it will lead to badly thought-out, spontaneous decisions which at best will do nothing and at worst will send you off in completely the wrong direction. Don't get me wrong; you never need 50 pages of a plan to try and follow, but at least a page of bullet points that you can share with your team or use yourself is essential.

5. Number neglect. Knowledge truly is power when it comes to the numbers in your business. If you don't know every aspect of your business from income per head, to customer count, to average purchase price, to profit, you are working blind. Look at all of your systems and rewire them so that you have this information to hand every minute of every working day. Remember, poor cash flow management is one of the biggest causes of business failure.

6. Carrying dead wood. No one likes to say it, but this is a syndrome most businesses are guilty of. There can be a range of reasons for this problem. Sometimes there is a slump and there are just too many bodies around to be viable. Other times, the numbers are OK, but staff have just failed to grow with your business. Then there are employees who are just plain obstructive. Many business owners hide behind the excuse that employment law 'is too draconian' to put off doing anything about staff changes. Ignorance of the real scope of employment law is no excuse though and there are clearly ways to shed staff if the reasons are right. If you are not sure what to do, engage an expert. It will be money well spent to map out a fair process.

7. Failure to embrace new technologies/developments. Things change. All the time. The businesses that come out on top are the ones that make the best use of new technologies and methods. If you don't, you will soon find yourself at a cost and marketing disadvantage to your more forward-thinking rivals. Your customers are going digital; so should you.

8. Self-stagnation. You don't know it all, however good you think you are. It is not enough to go with the flow and pick up skills along the way. You need to keep learning and developing your knowledge. The same goes for your staff. Start thinking about the gaps in your knowledge and how you can fill them in. (See 'Week 16: Knowledge partners - How to help staff to reach their full potential'). If you want to be the best, you have to work hard at it.

We all know that start-up businesses have as much as a one in three failure rate. The reverse of this is two out of three survive and go on to prosper. So, even if things look momentarily bleak, stay positive, check this guide, work out what your problem is (or are) and act fast to rewire your business.

Scribble your stuff here

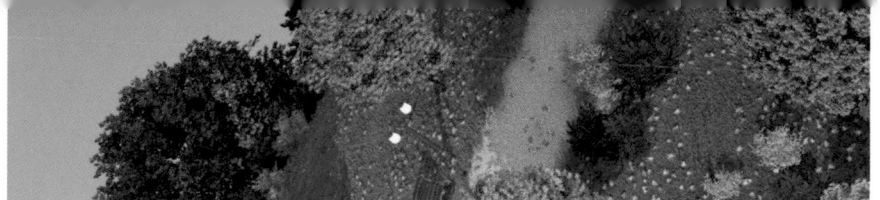

Week 39

Front Foot or Lose It - Keep a tight reign on everything. Always.

Not long ago, I started a life insurance broker under my same group structure. I put two of my trusted people in charge of the day-to-day activities and left them to get on with it.

It was a disaster. In the 10 months since it started trading, four out of the nine people employed by the company resigned. Plus, notwithstanding that this was essentially a start-up, profits at the business were nothing like they should be at the stage when I finally thought I had no choice but to intervene.

"What's going on?" I asked the guys who I had put in charge. "Why is this business not flying? It had such an amazing potential."

Looking at their panic-stricken faces, I quickly realised that the pair were completely stuck. Yes, stuck!

They had spent pretty much their entire time over five months reacting to what was going on. They were firefighting because they had lost so many employees. They were readjusting their plans because customers were not converting in high enough numbers or spending as much as expected. They were reviewing budgets because they may need to do some more marketing, as well as scaling back the income targets and projections.

To me, there is nothing worse than a company which reacts by contracting into its shell, and then cuts back in an apparently desperate bid to survive.

"Stop!" I said. "Stop, all this now. If you don't get on the front foot, you may as well not be here."

It's true. Unless you step forward and take control of a business situation, you will lose. If you want to run a successful business, you have to be proactive. It doesn't matter if things look a little daunting; you need to take control. Always.

My solution to this dilemma with my life insurance broker was to immediately take steps to scale up the business. I'd had enough of the strategy of trying to conserve cash and eke out a meagre profit. I wanted results.

"Scale it up," I told my business managers. "Go out and employ 20 people today. If you don't, the next employee who walks out will effectively kill this business for good. It is too weak to withstand this sort of disruption."

Once there are two dozen people on board, the business will move onto a different plane. Even looking at it on a very basic level, it is easy to see that; if a business is making £10,000 profit a month with nine people, it could make double that with 18 employees on the team. You should never be afraid to be proactive and to scale up.

Getting on the front foot is not rocket science. Like a lot of things in this diary, it is simply a question of having the balls to do it. But then again, if you don't, you'll probably not have picked up this book.

So, to be proactive, all you need to do is:

- **Know your priorities.** Making money is your number one priority, right? That is a given. So, how come business owners seem to forget it when day-to-day niggles throw them off course? Don't be too willing to bend with the prevailing wind, change your core strategy, or alter your objectives. We all know why we are here.

- **Tell everyone!** If you know what you want to achieve, tell everyone about it. It shouldn't be a secret. I don't mean that you say you want to make pots of cash and disappear off to an island in the sun. I mean that you emphasise to everyone around you that it is important to scale up the business, get things moving and make a big impact on your sector. You are not in it to coast along.

- **Tell everyone again.** And again. People forget. Just like the folks at my life insurance business; other things get in the way and distract them from what they should really be doing.

- **Invest.** Oh yes, the old speculate to accumulate mantra still does hold true. So, if it works, why not do it? Invest boldly in your business. Similarly, if a part of the business shows signs that it is doing well, or has potential to do so, put even more resources behind it. It'll build up the confidence in the team behind the 'good bit' and hopefully some of it might rub off on those involved in areas which are struggling.

- **Don't reinvent the wheel.** One of the main things that slow firms down is the need to constantly reinvent the wheel. It's almost impossible to get on the front foot if you always have to start from what seems like scratch. Put your best people on to any new project or venture, and let them share their expertise with the others.

- **Work!** Cut down on the meetings and other time consuming acts, which don't really move things on or solve anything. Instead, figure out what will really prompt a breakthrough in the firm (and don't be afraid to really go for it) and then do it.

- **Celebrate success.** When the team does start listening and gets on the front foot, don't forget to make a really big deal out of it. Make a fuss out of the people who have achieved results and made things motor. Apart from the fact that it demonstrates that you do value your priorities, it'll also temper your reputation as that grumpy boss who is always yelling about mistakes, failures and getting on the front foot!

If you want to be successful, you have to be proactive, not reactive. You, and the team, need to produce results, not excuses for failure. I'm not interested in why this or that didn't happen, or why so and so didn't achieve such and such. Nor should you be. Similarly, I don't want to 'act upon' potential problems. That is not going to get me anywhere.

The only way I am going to turn my potential into a reality is by getting on the front foot. Anything else is just for losers.

Create, not Dictate

Scribble your stuff here

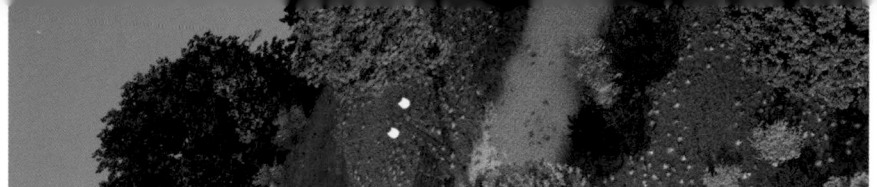

Week 40

Bad Customer Experiences -
Don't let them happen

Everyone has a 'hall of shame' tucked away in their minds, listing those companies which have given them truly appalling service. You know, an experience so bad it is imprinted on our brains and just the mere mention of the company will have us rolling our eyes, or shaking our heads in disbelief at the memory.

A couple of recent gems from my own personal hall of shame include:

- An electrician who had come to my house several times to do some quite substantial jobs, but on the most recent occasion he left, having left one small task undone. It took me a whole week to get hold of him and his reply as to when he might be back to finish the job was that he didn't need work that badly! Prior to that, there had been no cross words between us; I had always paid him on time and we had treated him well. In fact, the only thing he could possibly have complained about was my wife's coffee! I could only assume he had won the lottery in between times, because I thought trades people needed every job they could get their hands on in the current climate.

- I went to a large PC retailer (the clue to its identity is in the name) to buy myself a computer. The one I chose was on sale for £2,000 and I stood beside it patiently waiting for some service. After being ignored for 20 minutes by sales assistants who simply hurried by, I collared the sales manager and asked him for help. "I'll be with you shortly," he said briskly as he too passed by. I waited a further 15 minutes before approaching him again. I said, firmly but not unreasonably, "I have been waiting 35 minutes for someone to help me buy this PC." Do you know what he said? He said, "If you are going to be this impatient sir, you had better leave the premises!" Of course, I promptly left the building, never to return again.

Ask any group of people about their own personal customer services nightmares and the chances are, once they have named the offending company (or companies, more likely), there will be a barrage of comments like:

- They don't employ people who care
- They never listen
- They are more interested in their own systems

How would you feel if someone was saying this about your business? Amazingly, many companies don't seem to give this aspect of their business a second thought. Somehow, in the rush to scale up their venture, or introduce new products or working practices, they lose sight of the poor so-and-sos who actually buy the products. They are blissfully ignorant of things that drive their customers mad.

Then they agonise over the best thing they could do for their business to generate more revenue. Should they experiment with new technology? Or open new branches? Perhaps create a new division?

I feel like shouting, "Oi, look at the people you've got walking out the door! Shouldn't you be looking after them properly first?"

Apart from anything else, with today's tough global economy, you just can't afford to lose paying customers. Providing exceptional customer service is no longer an added benefit; it is a necessity. Customers who are not satisfied with the service they are getting can, and will, take their business elsewhere.

One of the most important things you could do for your business today is to build customer loyalty. Once you have a loyal customer, you will be the only shop/hotel/manufacturer/insurance business in the marketplace. None of your rival brands will come close. Your customers will only have eyes for you. That loyal customer will even do your marketing for you - for free - by telling everyone else about how fantastic you are.

Improving your customer service will give you:

- Competitive advantage - Competition is fierce in any industry. If you get things right and your competitors don't, which company is going to win more business?

- Cost-effectiveness - It costs five times as much to gain a new customer than to retain an existing one and keep them happy. The longer a company can keep a customer, the more money it will make.

- Higher efficiencies - When you focus on areas that directly affect customer satisfaction, you will utilise your resources more efficiently.

- Increased morale and satisfaction - Happy customers = a happy team.

The first step in sorting out your customer service is to find out what is important to your customers. It might sound completely obvious, but again you'd be amazed how many companies miss this bit out.

In the case of my PC experience above, what was important to me was being served in a timely and attentive manner. With other services, say an online company, it is delivery on time, or returning calls when they said they would. There are a myriad of demands on every company, all with differing importance in the eyes of the man on the street.

Put yourself in the shoes of your customers. What is it that you would expect from your business? What would be a priority for you. Then, ask yourself, "Is it happening?"

The other customer services basics I would make sure are going on as a matter of course are:

1. Answer the phone. Make sure that someone is always there to pick up the phone politely and attentively when a customer calls. Don't, if at all possible, use an automated service. No one likes talking to a robot and most of the time they give up before they get through.

2. Listen. Let your customers talk, and listen, really listen, to what they have to say. There is nothing more frustrating for a customer as when they carefully explain why things are wrong, only to realise the person on the other side has not logged a word.

3. Deal with complaints. Straight away. If you ignore a problem, it will only escalate. However, if you sort out someone's problem quickly and efficiently, you'll have a new ambassador for the company.

4. Be helpful - even if there is no immediate upside. If you are polite and helpful to a would-be customer, even if it does not result in a sale right there and then, who do you think they will come back to when they do have money to spend?

5. Keep your promises. Be reliable - nothing annoys a customer more than a broken promise.

Good customer service is not something you can deal with alone. It has to become part of the culture of the company and a priority for everyone on the team. Talk to them about how important it is to you and then keep reminding them. Make sure they are fully equipped to deal with problems, so they don't have to fob off a customer with "I don't know, but Mr. X will come back to you later."

Make it a rule that if anyone on the team picks up on a complaint, even if it is not anything to do with them, they must own that complaint and see it through to a successful conclusion.

Above all, remember that good customer service is not a one-day wonder. You must maintain the good work and keep the team on top of it too. Get it right and it will sustain the company through good times and bad for many years to come.

It's good to have the fear of loss

Scribble your stuff here

www.diaryofafortunehunter.com
Follow me on twitter@lyndonx

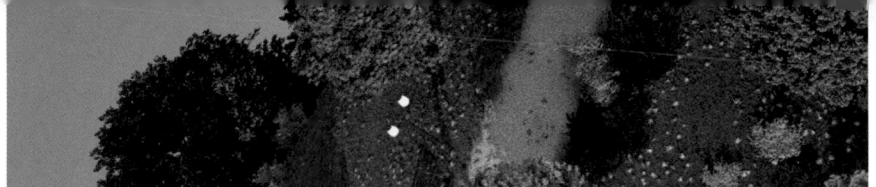

Week 41

Price Cutting is a Disaster

It's an unfortunate fact of life that we are in an era of bargain hunters and, with the economy going nowhere fast, this is not likely to change for a while to come. Daily deal sites like Groupon don't help the cause much either and put everyone into the mindset that it is possible to get massive discounts on just about anything.

It'll probably come as no surprise to you to hear that one of the questions I am most frequently asked by entrepreneurs in recent years is, "Should I cut my prices?"

My answer is, however, "Most definitely not!"

Cutting prices is a short term strategy and, in the wrong circumstances, can do real long term damage to your business. The only time you should consider discounts is when you have old stock to shift, or want to offer new customers a short term incentive.

Price reductions are not a Band-Aid, or miracle cure, for times when your bottom line is haemorrhaging. They will simply weaken the business and damage its long term profitability.

Why?

1.   **Even the smallest cuts have big consequences.**
        If you cut your prices, even by a few pence, you will have to produce a significant increase in sales, just to maintain the same profit level as before the cuts. You will need a powerful (and possibly expensive) marketing strategy in place to get the extra sales required.

2.   **You open yourself up to counter-attacks.**
        Aside from the fact that price cuts have to be accompanied by real cost reductions in your manufacturing or supply base - otherwise you will be eroding your profit - they also open you up to the possibility that your competitors will do just the same. If they do this, are you going to keep on cutting costs? How long could you keep that up?

3. **Consumers will begin to question the quality of your product/service.**
   We all know that you don't get something for nothing. If you cut your prices significantly, your customers will start to scrutinise your offering more closely. Your product may not have changed one jot, but your customers may feel less satisfied, or even complain more.

4. **Customers could see it as a panic measure.**
   The last thing you want is a drop in confidence around your firm because consumers may cast around elsewhere, in case you are not around tomorrow.

5. **Customers have short memories.**
   Customers will get used to the new, lower price very quickly. In fact, pretty soon, it will feel like the 'right' price. Raising your prices to their 'normal' level after a prolonged cut is not an easy strategy to pull off.

6. **If you promote yourself as cheap, you will never, ever, shake the moniker.**
   The only way to carry on will be to constantly reduce prices and stay below the competition. This is, of course, an utterly unsustainable strategy for most small and medium sized businesses that will be constantly at the mercy of bigger players with greater purchasing power.

So, what can you do? The fact that everyone wants more for less cannot be ignored. Plus, if you don't offer your customers something pretty special, someone else will.

The answer is, don't reduce the price of your core products. Instead, offer your customers more value.

Perceived value is all about how your customers see what you sell and their own expectations on the economic and psychological benefits they get from it. It is much better to add value to your existing products by improving the way people view them, instead of slashing prices in a desperate bid to hold on to customers.

In short, if you want your product to be twice as valuable, don't cut your prices in half, double the value of what you provide.

Ideas you may like to consider are:

1. **Create a new tier of products and services.**
   This group of products - which will be sold entirely separately from your usual range - will be sold at a new, lower, price but will clearly offer less bells and whistles than your flagship range. Customers will see that you recognise budgets are tight and will have the option of upgrading to their higher spec product when the economy recovers. This is an extension of the strategy employed by airlines of 'first class', 'business class' and 'economy'.

2. **Segment products and prices according to time, location or quantity.**
   Similar to the above, create a new tier of products according to when or where they are bought i.e. off peak, or peak. This may not suit every business, but the more you can slice and dice your prices without affecting your core brand, the better.

3. **Bundle products.**
   Put together a new package of all your products. If customers upgrade to buy them all at the same time, they will be rewarded with a 10 per cent discount.

4. **Pamper loyal customers.**
   Keep your best customers happy with loyalty programmes, or adding the occasional extra. If you sell shirts at £80 each, for example, add in a free tie that normally retails at £30. The tie itself will only have cost you £10 wholesale, but your customer will be blown away by the apparent £30 freebie. Business to business firms may like to offer training to their loyal customers. It won't just add perceived value; it will also make it more difficult for them to switch to another provider.

5. **Stick to your guns.**
   When times are tough, sales forces often become less resistant to customer pressures. They'll knock down the price until the sale is won. Arm them with all the new bundles and packages you have created to add to the perceived value and draw the line in the sand about how low you will let your prices go. If they resist, find some way to encourage them to stick to that level. This may well entail introducing a new bonus structure which is not based entirely on sales volume.

It is always natural at times like this to keep one eye on what competitors are doing and react accordingly. However, I would strongly resist the urge to simply slash prices to remain in the game. Creating bundles of products, segmenting the market and looking after loyal customers are the right ways to win the price war without bringing your company to its knees. Knee-jerk price cuts are a mug's game.

Scribble your stuff here

Week 42

Cornered Options - Don't become reliant on too few suppliers

One of my prime philosophies in my business life is to always, always keep my options open. I hate being backed into a corner. I know that if I don't do something about something that niggles me or boxes me in, it will, at some stage, bite me on the arse.

The most common cause of this syndrome is when a business becomes too reliant on a single supplier. Invariably, this is a recipe for disaster. So many things can go wrong. If the supplier goes out of business, you are stuffed. Overnight you will be left high and dry without whatever component they supplied you with (not to mention you'll probably be hugely out of pocket). You're also stuffed if the supplier becomes lax, or complacent. Suddenly, through no fault of your own, the quality of your business will plummet.

I've found myself in this sort of situation a few times, and have always changed things the moment I realise that I have become cornered.

The first time I became aware of it was when I weighed up my firm's relationship with the software house which had developed our systems for more than a decade. I had worked with them from the early days, but it was becoming apparent to me that we had outgrown them. As my business had got bigger, our IT requirements had become more and more complex. We were at a stage where our software partner could lick-and-stick a few add-ons to keep us going, but it was by no means a satisfactory, long term, solution and it kept crashing with countless hours of downtime. Yet, this firm had practically our entire infrastructure in their hands. If we wanted to change our supplier, we would have to start from scratch and that was no small undertaking. It would be a huge financial investment.

I had a choice. I could carry on being reliant on this supplier and limp along with all the dangers that came with it. Or I could swallow the investment and move on.

I, of course, followed the latter course taking on a large software house and also, by way of belt and braces, bought a lot of the development in-house to spread the reliance. I was no longer backed into a corner by my software developer.

This situation can also play out within your company too. If you employ a specialist who has a level of knowledge about some aspect of the business that no one else does, this can also force you into a corner. Ironically, my instance of this is also in the field of software. The person involved held all the cards because he knew how to code our system inside out and upside down. Unfortunately, no one else in the firm had anything like this depth of understanding and it made me feel incredibly vulnerable. After all, there is no way I could discipline this person if he did anything wrong. I would just have to sit there and take it.

What did I do? Well, I didn't become a coder! I went out into the market and sought out technology solutions which I could bring in at a moment's notice as and when I needed them. That brought immediate peace of mind.

As a business owner, there is nothing worse than feeling restrained, cornered or reliant on something or someone else. Companies go bust by not giving themselves options. Apart from anything else, you set up business to be free from this sort of nonsense.

Check out if your business is too reliant on specific suppliers by answering the following questions about your firm and its key suppliers:

1.   Is the product or service absolutely vital to your operation? In my case, software is a key part of the smooth running of my business. Alternatively, if you are a furniture builder, then your lumber supplier will be pretty important. On the other hand, office supplies are not something that is essential to your business. You could quite easily get a ream of foolscap elsewhere if your local office supply store goes under.

2. Is the product or service only provided by a small set of suppliers? There are very few companies which have a monopoly on a particular product, however there are some specialty items (such as bespoke software) which will only be sold or made by a specific company. If this is the case with your firm, you could be in big trouble if things change.

3. Is the product or service based on a binding partnership or strategic agreement? Here I am talking about examples such as a restaurant that agrees to only sell drinks supplied by one beverage company. If the partnership goes sour, you could easily face delays in sourcing other drinks. This sort of thing can put your core business strategy in danger.

4. Is your business model based on selling only specific brand name products? If the supplier of these brands has a change of heart, your shelves are going to be pretty empty.

5. Are there, as in my case, key employees who would leave a huge hole in your operation if they left because they have very specific, specialised knowledge?

If, by answering these questions, you can see that your business is at risk, you should take steps to minimise your dependence.

The first, and most obvious, step is to seek multiple alternatives. You don't need to switch to them immediately, or even ever, but it will give you peace of mind. If you know the delivery terms and price structure of the alternative suppliers, you'll be able to hit the ground running if and when you need to. You may, however, like to try a few trial orders with the alternative suppliers. It will help in building a business relationship that will make any transition easier later on.

Apart from the fact it will help you feel less cornered, it is a lot easier to react in a crisis when you've already done your homework.

You may also like to consider the agreements you have with your existing supplier if you are so inexorably tied to them. Talk to legal advisors about setting up more concrete long term agreements, which will safeguard your interests. Bear in mind that this won't be worth a can of beans if your supplier goes bust.

In addition, you may like to think about bringing some functions in-house as I did. There are, of course, the usual provisos about not getting too tied down with your own expert, but having experts on-site should be more manageable and give you greater control.

Setting up a lot of these measures may seem like quite an onerous task - particularly when things are bumping along OK. But, if you don't think ahead, you shouldn't be in business and probably won't be for too long.

If you want to protect what you are building, don't let yourself get cornered.

Scribble your stuff here

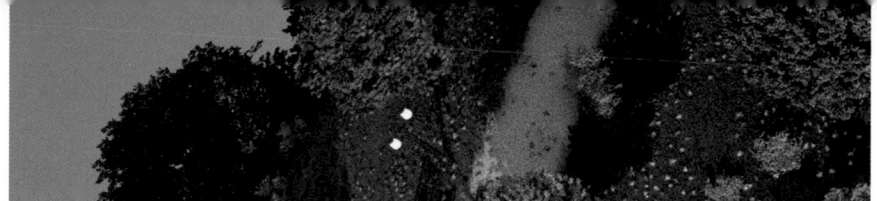

Week 43

Brain invaders -
Set priorities and stick to them

My wife was eager to start her own business and I, ever keen to support any entrepreneurial activity as well as my family, helped her set up her own spa. The Chocolate Salon Spa in Cardiff was a luxurious affair, offering all sorts of top-notch treatments from Microdermabrasion to aromatherapy massage. To anyone on the outside, it was a lovely little thriving business. Except it wasn't.

As I very quickly discovered, it was a very time-consuming venture to run and the smallest thing could throw it off track. The diary could be full, for example, and then one of the ladies who did the treatments would call in sick and everything would be thrown into chaos. Or someone would hand in their notice and it would take weeks and weeks to find a qualified expert in the area to replace them. There were seemingly endless possibilities as to what could go wrong and a great deal did.

Very soon, I was spending many hours each day helping my wife sort out the almost daily crises and daily duties. We would both be up late into the night, pouring over diaries and spreadsheets, and the next day would always invariably bring in a new horror. This was, of course, on top of my 'day job' dealing with my various business interests.

Eventually, I thought, enough is enough. What am I doing? This doesn't make sense. If I am not actually physically working through the Chocolate Salon Spa's problems, I am thinking about them. If I am not thinking about them, I am discussing what to do about them with my wife and having heated debates. My brain space was completely and utterly consumed by this tiny lifestyle business.

So, I sat down to look at the figures.

Here was a business that was losing my family an average of £2,000 a month. Yet, it was taking up about 30 per cent of my time and probably about 70 per cent of my thoughts.

Yet, my insurance businesses, which bring me more than £600,000 a month, were only getting 70 per cent of my effort and less than 30 per cent of my brain space. In reality, I was starting to let them just tick along.

If I decided to really go for it with the Chocolate Salon Spa and devoted even more of my time and brain space to the venture, I estimated that, at best, I could only turn a £1,000 per month profit from the business. Meanwhile, having taken the eye off the ball even more at my main business, my profit could easily have dropped to £500,000 a month.

When you look at the spa business in these terms, it simply does not make any sense at all. I could make at least one hundred times as much out of my insurance companies, with less effort. If I was freed to concentrate solely on my main business, think how much more money I could make too. So, with my wife's full blessing and after two years of trying, we pulled the plug on the Chocolate Salon Spa. It was the only logical thing to do.

This is perhaps an extreme example, but I think we all suffer from letting peripheral stuff take over our brain to distract us from our main businesses. These brain invaders, as I call them, can come from anywhere. They could be a troublesome sideline, like the Chocolate Salon Spa, or a tricky personal relationship, or even an all-consuming hobby. However, if you want to make money, you cannot afford to let these things distract you and take your eye off the main prize.

It is a natural human reaction to ignore the time wasted on thinking about things that, at the end of the day, don't really matter. Yes, it might seem like a big deal at the time, but if you break it down like I have here, it is very easy to see what a fool you are being.

Don't let it happen to you.

Do an audit of what is taking up your brain space. Is it your business? Or is something else preoccupying you? Is that something that is preoccupying you worth the time and trouble? Is it as important as your business? Really?

When there is something invading your brain, don't ignore it. Sort it out, resolve it or get rid of it. True fortune hunters only ever expend their energy and brainpower where there is an opportunity for maximum returns.

There is, however, an important proviso here. Don't be so ruthless in concentrating entirely on your current business and protecting your brain space that you shut out all other thoughts and ideas. After all, today's distraction could be the beginnings of tomorrow's multi-million pound idea. Twitter, after all, started off as a side project at Odeo. Starbucks started off selling beans and coffee makers, with no interest in brewing up your skinny Cappuccinos. Fortune hunters just need to learn to differentiate between the distractions and the potential game changers.

So, if you find yourself increasingly preoccupied with something other than your main business, ask yourself the following questions:

- How big is the potential market for this thing that is taking up my brain space?

- How much of my brain space would I need to devote to it in order to realise the potential market?

- Am I the right person to be developing this idea, or is it so far away from my current skill set that I am actually just wasting my time?

- Does this preoccupation dovetail with my existing business in any way? Could I cross-sell it to my existing customers? Or, could it actually harm my existing business?

- How much am I harming my existing business by devoting so much time to this brain invader?

- Why am I even considering this?

- Is it a scalable business or just a lifestyle one?

- Is it just EGO, or a real opportunity?

If you answer these questions honestly, you will have a clearer idea of the motivation behind this thing that has invaded your brain. If it looks like a goer, give it some more space. Put some plans in place and start making it a reality. If in all likelihood it is unlikely to ever be a money-maker, let it go.

If you start tackling all your brain invaders like this, very soon, with intuition and experience, you get to learn extremely quickly what is worth spending time on and what is not.

Use your brain space to tackle the things that will make you the most money. It will pay dividends.

Empower your sales team to dealmake and trade

Scribble your stuff here

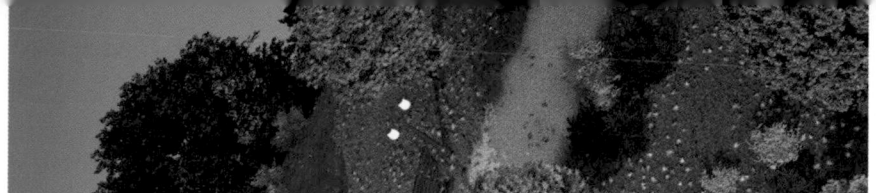

Week 44

Control your randoms -
Ignoring distractions

Distractions in a business begin the moment you take on your first member of staff. Initially, this new person will embody all your hopes, dreams and ambitions for the future and show you that your business is going places. If all is going well, that one person will multiply into two, then four and then eight then one hundred. It'll be like the Magician's Nephew, with staff popping up all over the place.

Then, you will have the microwave conversation. I guarantee it. The microwave conversation goes something like this:

"Boss, can we have a microwave for the staff room?"

"OK," you'll say, and you'll go out and buy one.

Then, you'll notice the microwave is constantly filthy because your team doesn't care about what it has taken to provide them with such amenities. It will drive you to distraction, because you know how hard you have had to work to get this far (yes, I know it is only a microwave, but you get the idea). So, after a few weeks of leaving exasperated notes asking people to clean up after themselves, you'll take it away. Pretty soon, a new wave of staff will come in and before you know it someone will ask, "Boss, can we have a microwave?"

And, so it goes on.

There are dozens of 'microwave issues' in companies large and small. They are annoying, time-consuming and drive you to distraction. While you are getting exasperated about these random, essentially inconsequential issues, important things are being ignored. Big decisions get neglected while you are looking the other way getting increasingly stressed and frustrated by petty requests and niggles.

You might think, "Hey, I am really busy!" You are not; you are simply being consumed by the wrong things. The little tasks are keeping you from achieving big things.

Distractions can come in many forms from your own pet hates (obviously, mine is the microwave situation), to constant interruptions to talk about things you have already dealt with. You must always take care to control them. Even simply taking time to think about them is costly to the business, rather like the driver who spends a few moments pondering whether to make a phone call when hurtling down the M1. Even that brief moment of lack of concentration can prove dangerous. You're unlikely to cause any fatal injuries from the safety of your office, but you could well end up losing your fortune because you are looking the wrong way.

Hard though it may seem, you, as a business leader, have to learn how to control your randoms.

The good news is, with a little discipline, it is not as difficult as you might think to do this. You, as a business owner and fellow fortune hunter are, after all, in charge of your own destiny. The key is to organise yourself better so you can focus on what counts and ignore the distractions. If you focus on your goals, you will not be so easily sidetracked by all the other things that bombard you every day.

There are several ways to do this:

- Remind yourself - time is money. Yes, time is a medium of exchange, just like money. We all exchange our time for money and if you are running your own show, every second of your time should be worth a great deal. Make a rough calculation of how much your time is worth per hour in fiscal terms. If it is, say, £2,000, should you be wasting a quarter of an hour, or £500, arguing the toss over a dirty microwave?

- Prioritise. You are not Superman, or Superwoman. There are a finite number of things you can do in a day. One of the prime causes of failure is trying to do too many things at a time. Generally, trying to do too many things at once means nothing gets done. Or, at the very least, not much gets done properly. So, break your goals down into order, work out which ones are the most important and assign an appropriate amount of time to each one. The microwave conversation should be at the bottom of this list, somewhere below emptying the wastepaper bins and choosing the colour of the office coffee cups.

- Change the structure of your day. When you run a business you will constantly be bombarded with all sorts of random requests from accounts, from HR, from the sales team; everywhere are emails, texts, chats, letters, conversations and debates. Find a new structure in your day so that you set aside, say an hour a day to review all these requests and that is it. Don't just immediately respond to every email, phone call and knock on the door. It will distract you from the job in hand and nothing will get done properly.

- Let people vent - but not over and over again. Leaders need to let employees express their point of view or the team will get angry and feel disenfranchised. But, once they are done, agree what will happen next and declare the matter closed. Once a decision is made, everyone must move forward. Don't spend hours, or even weeks, going over old ground.

- Give the team ownership. You don't have to, indeed can't, deal with every little issue. Ensure that everyone knows that your door and email inbox are always open, but encourage an atmosphere where everyone shapes at least some changes for themselves. Obviously, you will be the first to intervene if a little issue looks like turning into a big one, but challenge the team to come up with their own solutions.

There is, however, one important caveat to controlling your randoms. Keep an eye on the fact that, now and again, little issues are not really little issues at all. They are symptomatic of something going very wrong. However, the little issues are just seized upon by those who are resistant to other changes in the firm. So, for example, if a team is up in arms about a shift in lunch hour times, it might not be that they really care about what time they eat their sandwiches; it might simply be that they are scared of a new boss, or a new management system, or maybe it was not communicated well to them.

So, be vigilant, keep an eye on the subtext, but do not let every little niggle drive you round the bend and distract you from the important business of making money.

Scribble your stuff here

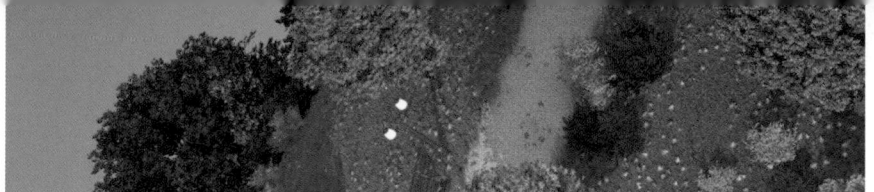

Week 45

Time Theft - And don't let the team get distracted either!

Whether it is cyberslacking, or gossiping by the photocopier, or flirtations by the water cooler, witnessing examples of employee time-wasting has to be one of the most frustrating sights to confront a fortune hunter. There you are, working your butt off to make your business a success and when you look around the room, all you can see is people cruising social networks on their computer, or looking for holiday deals online, or repeatedly wandering off to the loo.

Time theft is utterly maddening and it can seriously affect your bottom line. Employees who don't commit fully to their jobs leave a backlog of work for their co-workers to mop up, or force you to pay overtime so they can complete the tasks they have already been paid for. Time thieves increase your costs and reduce your profits.

It happens everywhere. According to research, 22 per cent of employees admitted to wasting around two hours a day, while 14 per cent confessed to slacking for more than three hours. That is more than one third of workers wasting two hours every single workday!

To see how much this was costing me, I did a back-of-the-envelope calculation in my own firm to establish the true cost of time theft. You can try it too:

1. Divide your turnover by 365 working days (if your business is a five day week operation, divide by 252). You now have a rough approximation of how much your firm earns per working day.

2. Divide this figure by the number of employees on the payroll to get a rough estimation of each person's 'share' of earning that income.

3. Divide the daily earnings of each employee by seven (assuming a seven hour working day). This figure will show you how much per hour of wasted time this is costing.

4. You could also further divide the figure by 60, to find out how much you are losing per minute.

This is obviously a very rough calculation and does not take into account the differences in salary and position. However, this exercise showed me that every wasted minute by each employee was costing me £58. Yes, that is £58!

It is a bit of an eye-opener, I can tell you. It certainly changes your perspective when you watch one member of staff take 20 minutes to photocopy one sheet, while discussing last night's episode of *EastEnders*. In that time, I'd have just burned £1,160! It focuses your mind a bit, I can tell you.

Taking this one step further, I started to probe into what my staff were doing at their desks. I started in my call centre. Using our systems to examine their work rate (basically the gaps when they were not making calls), I could surmise that each person was active on calls for just five out of the seven hours of the working day they were being paid for. This translated into a time theft loss of around £7,000 per day, for the two hours wasted doing god knows what.

As an employer, I have to be realistic. Staff are people, not robots. It would be a pretty dull office if no one had a chat now and again, and interaction is important to pass on information and share knowledge. Plus I can't really complain about my staff nipping to the loo. There does, however, need to be an element of give and take. My team is paid well to do a good job and I don't like them taking the piss.

To find a solution, I looked at the issue more deeply. What I found was that there were three sorts of time-wasting:

- *Deliberate*. Mercifully rare, these are the people who hate their job, their employer and probably the world, and set out to take something back from their firm. It's usually symptomatic of a complete breakdown of trust in the employer and employee relationship and has to be nipped in the bud immediately because it is hugely distracting to everyone else.

- *Conscious*. This is when an employee takes time out to attend to something other than work, such as looking after their personal needs, like internet shopping or booking a holiday. It is not a malicious act on the behalf of the employee. They've simply made a judgement that the non-work activity is more important (and they're going to be paid anyway).

- *Unconscious*. Generally a result of inefficient work practices, poor processes and bad time management. Your technology may be out-dated, or your training scheme out of touch with the job in hand. What this means is that staff are unable to realise their true potential because they have not got all the tools to do their job with the utmost efficiency. Another symptom of unconscious time-wasting is a culture of time consuming, yet ineffective, meetings.

Of the three causes of time-wasting, the first and the third are probably the most easy to fix. Disgruntled employees clearly cannot be left to fester, and must be identified and dealt with. You should also thoroughly examine your technology, systems and processes to ensure you are getting the optimum use from them. Meetings can also be reorganised (and preferably reduced) to give them some structure.

The conscious time-wasting element requires more time and energy to put right. My starting point is to be utterly transparent with my team. I showed them the time theft calculation that I did here to show them how destructive it could be. After all, if the company makes less profit at the end of the year, it means lower pay increases and reduced bonus for them. After all, they have a stake in the success of this company too.

I didn't let it drop off the agenda either. From that time on, whenever I have discussed performance and results, I have always referred to the destructiveness of time theft.

By way of compromise, and to give the team a little leeway, I agreed to organise opportunities for social interaction at work, such as company-wide events. These events are always scheduled during normal business hours, as opposed to after work, to send the message that they are a priority.

Finally, I ensured that the senior managers and I set a good example. Like so many work issues, if staff sees the top team constantly slacking, or larking around, it is very likely they'll take this as their cue. Clearly, if you don't take time management seriously, it is pretty unlikely that those around you are going to carry on working their socks off. So, keep away from the water cooler - it will save you tens of thousands of pounds!

Scribble your stuff here

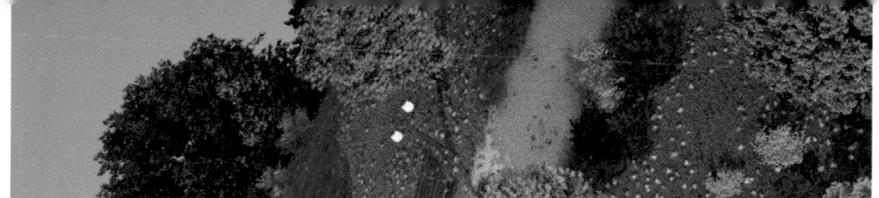

Week 46

Perception & Reality -
Making informed decisions

I was recently invited to attend a Business Lounge dinner in Cardiff, which is an exclusive event for company owners, managing directors and CEOs. As I have said many times in this book, I value my time greatly and as a rule try to limit the amount of networking events I go to. So I replied with a polite letter asking for an attendee list to see if it was worth my while.

The organisers replied by return and said that regretfully they were unable to give me such a list because the event was being run under Chatham House Rules. (For those that don't know this - and I didn't - this means it is run on the condition of anonymity to encourage openness and the sharing of information)

I decided that if I didn't know more about how I would be spending my time, who with, or how valuable it would be to me, I would give it a miss. I wrote the organisers a pleasant email, thanking them for the invite, but adding that I was unable to attend because I value my time. I added, perhaps rather cheekily, that it gave me an idea for a chapter for my book!

That idea was that it is all too easy to get carried away by the perception of things and ignore the reality. I could have easily got swept up in the prestige of being invited to a senior business person's networking event, yet ignored the reality that it could, quite possibly, have wasted a few hours of my valuable time.

It got me thinking about all the other instances where you get emotionally wound up in things and see the world in one way, yet the actual real picture is somewhat different. You make a snap decision, based on what you see, whereas what you should really be doing is delving more deeply and finding out more about the true picture.

Funnily enough, at almost the same time as this was going on, I started getting some niggles from one of my admin departments. They appeared to be indicating that they were swept off their feet with work, which was why certain things were not happening. "There are far too many documents to prints, emails to send and stuff to post," they said. "We need more help."

AUTUMN - TROUBLESHOOTING

Instead of dashing off to recruit more bodies, or authorise overtime, I decided to delve into it more deeply. Yes, on face value, they did seem to have a lot to do. However, when I scrutinised the detail, the reality was far different. It turned out there were a manageable amount of documents to process, indeed, there were possibly far less than I had imagined. There were, however, some small problems with some of the systems that were slowing things down. I got those systems fixed and, hey presto, things were immediately running smoothly.

There are dozens of instances like this in every business, both internally and externally. You think you absolutely know something for sure, but the reality is completely different.

On a small scale, such as with this business networking event, it doesn't matter much. If I had gone along with high expectations and then found out it was stuffed full with second-raters (and I mean that with the greatest of respect), I will have only wasted a few hours (although those hours do add up). However, what happens if this is happening on a grand scale? What happens if there is a complete disconnect between your perceptions and those of your team, or, even worse, your customers?

You may, for example, think that everyone sees you as this young, go-getting, exciting business, when they actually think of you as sluggish and a bit behind the times. If you just stick to the 'truth' as you see it, you will sail on in your own sweet way, wasting time on things you shouldn't, while missing some vital opportunities.

If you don't constantly repeat the mantra 'perception or reality', you could come unstuck and make some really stupid, knee-jerk, decisions based on what you think you understand. What you should be doing as an entrepreneur is basing all of your decisions on hard facts.

It is vital to know if there are gaps between your customers' experience and what you are delivering. Similarly, you must be comfortable that your whole team is on-target, on-message and working as you expect.

The key to all this is to ask questions. All the time. This may sound simple, but sometimes people are reluctant to raise what might be an uncomfortable truth. If they have an inkling that they may not like to hear the answer - or deal with it - it is easier to let sleeping dogs lie.

Don't be afraid either if any of the questions seem awkward. Most people don't mind a bit of straight talking and to be honest, even if they do, who cares? You need to know what you are dealing with. Listen to your intuition too. If something doesn't feel right, it probably isn't. That is the cue to get in as much data as you can lay your hands on to test your thinking.

I've never agreed with that saying 'don't sweat the small stuff'. If you are not demanding and don't delve into things, you could easily end up needlessly wasting your time, or heading off in the wrong direction. And, as we all know, ignoring the little things only leaves them to grow into big problems. I know from experience that there is nothing that gets me more frustrated and angry than when I missed something because I thought it was all fine. I get over that by constantly reminding myself; perception and reality.

As an afterthought, I ought to mention that the organiser of the event responded rather well to my persistent questioning. She eventually waived the fee of the event in order to get me there to see it for myself. Of course, I can't tell you whether it was of value or not, as I am bound by Chatham House Rules!

Maximise and dominate distribution

Scribble your stuff here

_____

_____

_____

_____

_____

_____

_____

_____

_____

_____

_____

_____

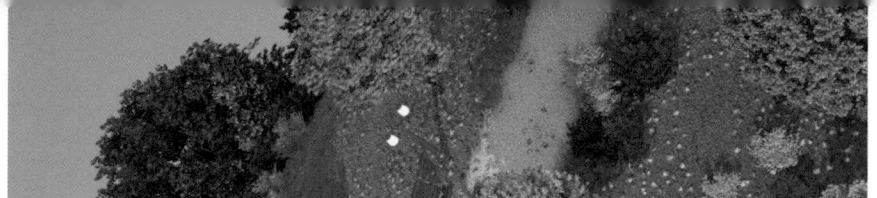

Week 47

It's not about what you see, it is what you can't see - Buying another business

In late 2001, my fledgling insurance business was on its knees. Following the Twin Tower terrorist attacks of September 11, the entire insurance industry was suffering and my firm was no exception. The major player that I worked with to place my policies were paring back their business and only sticking with their most profitable accounts. My account was profitable, but not the most profitable, so suddenly they stopped dealing with me and almost overnight I lost 45 per cent of my clients. I was simply unable to renew my clients' policies in partnership with these highly cautious insurance giants.

For a while, I felt like my brain had snapped in two. I was employing 35 staff, had heavy financial commitments in terms of mortgage on the offices and wages, and big ambitions for the future. Yet my business had ground to a virtual halt. After weighing up whether to jack it all in and start elsewhere, perhaps even in an entirely new sector, I decided the solution was to buy a brokerage. If I could do this, it would give me unfettered access to the big insurance agencies such as Aviva, Axa and so on, which would in turn kick-start my recovery from this perilous situation.

Having made up my mind, I ended up buying a small broker in Liverpool for £120,000 in eight days flat after conducting virtually no due diligence. This brokerage had a head office (which is the one I acquired) and five small branches, and I paid cash up front and signed an A4 agreement. This move pretty much flies in the face of any small business guide and is the sort of thing that would get most bank managers shaking their heads in despair.

Why did I do it?

Firstly, I am not a bank manager; I am a fortune hunter.

Secondly, if I hadn't done something, I was not likely to be in business much longer.

This acquisition wasn't the easiest of moves to make and it certainly did not emerge as an overnight success story. As it turned out, the seller was a bit of a crook and must have thought all his Christmases had come at once when I waived the customary lengthy checks. Sure enough, as soon as I got the keys to the door, I got slapped with a £60,000 liability for two tribunals which had been outstanding for over a year. That's outstanding for a year before I had even clapped eyes on the place! Clearly I had no choice but to settle the claims; even though they were not anything to do with me, the law was on their side. I had to drag out the negotiations as long as I could because I couldn't afford to fork out for them after buying the broker. But, as soon as I could raise the extra cash, I paid up.

In the end, although it was a struggle for a while, the brokerage turned out to be the best thing I could have done for my business. That's probably just as well, as I had precious few options at the time.

Since that time, I have bought another business to bolt on to my insurance firm and, looking back, can see that I have learned quite a few lessons from my experiences. My view is; it doesn't matter how good your due diligence is, or your acquisition process - buying any business is never straightforward. The odds are always stacked against you, whether you do it in eight days, or eight months. Why? Well, businesses are simply not designed to be easily acquired and integrated into other businesses. It is very hard, some would say well nigh impossible, to put together two businesses smoothly. The key is to think about this process long before you get the keys to the door.

It is for this reason that I would always pause and do a very thorough sense check before buying any business. It is very easy to get carried away by the heat of the moment and get talked into a great deal, which turns out to be anything but. So, stop and ask yourself, "Why am I buying this? Am I prepared for the aggravation?" And answer very honestly.

Remember, any acquisition will take up a number of man hours and tie up key members of your team who may be needed elsewhere, not to mention diverting your own attention from your core business. Does this acquisition really warrant this attention? Would your time be better employed elsewhere?

I would also think very carefully about the advisors you employ. Clearly, it makes total sense to use lawyers and advisors who are used to this kind of work (you'd be amazed how many companies don't) but don't get complacent. You are buying this business as part of your strategy, so get stuck in to some of the legwork yourself. If you leave it all down to your legal team, you will be exposed. I've often found that the paper trail around an acquisition will tell me one thing, but if I go out and talk to people, it will reveal something entirely different. Numbers and contracts are all very well, but it is the things that you can't immediately see that make all the difference. This personal due diligence also represents a great opportunity to winkle out any erstwhile hidden opportunities that you can explode the day you take over.

Finally, the secret to any good dealmaking is to always be prepared to walk away if something does not look right. I don't mean as a pseudo bargaining chip to force the price down; I mean to really be prepared to cut your losses if anything doesn't quite add up. Don't let your ego talk you into signing on the dotted line because you get carried away by the potential kudos behind making the deal. Adopt non-committal attitude, mean it and do it. Yes, if the deal goes sour, you'll lose a bit of cash and it will be annoying. However, it is better to walk away and find a better prospect elsewhere than be saddled with a nightmare business which is causing you trouble before you have even bought it.

If you get all of this right and there is a great fit between the businesses you put together, you will have made a great start. Of course, any deal is only as good as what you do next. There is no point doing the deal, shelling out the cash and basking in the glory of your growing empire. This is where the hard work begins and you focus on making it happen. Fight distractions, ambiguities and the naysayers and carry on making relentless progress towards your goals.

Summary

Every business is unique. Different problems will arise that will effect different companies, depending on the sector you are in. In this section I have shown just some of the most common problems that may arise and shown some of the actions you need to take to head them off. You may, however, encounter some entirely new and business-threatening situations. No challenge should prove fatal though, as long as you stay vigilant. The most important thing is that you stay aware and question everything. Every day.

AUTUMN - TROUBLESHOOTING

WINTER

This is the moment you have been waiting for – the time to realise the fruits of your hard work and finally reap your fortune.

Letting go of a business you have worked so hard to build up is never easy, but always remember why you started it in the first place: to make your fortune. If you judge that the time is right, now is the time to sell your business and achieve your dream.

Scribble your stuff here

Week 48

Focus on an exit

A few years ago, I decided to attempt to exit my business by putting it up for sale. A buyer was found, advisors were called in and we started the exhausting process of due diligence. In a short space of time, we had generated a pile of papers that must have been three foot high and I am not exaggerating.

Wading through these papers and answering the growing list of questions batted back and forth by the advisors, I had an epiphany. I realised that in those long hard years building up my successful business, I had lost sight of one of the most important goals there can be. I hadn't thought of the end game. I hadn't planned an exit. Needless to say, the sale fell through.

In the analysis that followed, I decided that:

- I had not been clear enough about the direction of my business, particularly with a view to its eventual sale.

- I had allowed an imbalance between the various sectors of my business and not really considered which parts would appeal to buyers. So, for example, the wholesale division was effectively propping up the retail side, but the market was only really interested in retail.

In my haste to grow the business, I had completely missed the point. If you want to be a successful fortune hunter, everything you do, every day, has to be completely focused on the exit, even if you do not plan to exit in the very near future. The exit is, of course, when you will realise the big payout.

Most people who buy businesses want to see a company which is well run, cost-efficient and with plenty of growth potential (unless the buyer is a restructuring specialist - but if your business is going in a fire sale, then you are not going to be getting a fortune any time soon). The aim of the game for the business seller is to maximise the value of your company, before converting it into hard cash. This means taking positive steps to maximise your pre-tax profits and future earnings.

For an entrepreneur, this can entail a whole new way of thinking. Concentrating on an exit means curbing some of your more creative ideas, your desire to innovate and the constant hankering to do new and exciting things with the business. Part of me is always thinking about investment to grow my company to the level I have always had a vision for. But, dull though it may be to give all this up, you have to remember that this is not the way to maximise the sales value of your firm.

To secure the exit valuation you deserve, you need to fill the EBITDA (earnings before income, tax, depreciation and amortisation). It is very easy to make a wrong move and significantly erode EBITDA if you are not on the ball. For example, if I invested £500,000 on something for my business, but it only produced an immediate return of £300,000, then I will have taken £200,000 out of my EBITDA and damaged my sought-after valuation. Like I say, it's frustrating to curb that entrepreneurial spirit, but it is a necessary evil if a sale is in your sights.

So, to concentrate my mind, I set myself 10 rules for running the business with a trade sale exit as the goal. If and when I choose to sell, I will follow these rules at least 12 to 24 months before I even consider activating the sale. The longer you groom your business, the greater the benefit. The rules are:

- **Manage costs tightly.** Don't get carried away spending money on your various divisions with one eye on hypergrowth. Start thinking in terms of the end game and ask yourself whether you really need that new person, or to replace equipment, or whether it would be better keeping things lean.

- **Manage your space.** Do you really need the luxury of all that office space or is it there just in case you outgrow it? Don't forget you are paying for the privilege of those empty desks.

- **Check your infrastructure.** As the business grows, it is tempting to recruit different teams for each section. Is this the most efficient use of your resources though? It may be that one manager could easily do the job of two across separate divisions, and it would make the business more efficient and saleable.

- **Do your research.** What deals are being done in your market right now? Who are the buyers and what are they buying? This is an important precursor to the next step.

- **Identify problem areas.** Take a long, hard, detached look at your business and identify which areas might be unattractive to would-be buyers. Now is the time to make decisions on what assets to keep and which ones should be wound down. Unwanted parts of the business will extend the timeframe of any sale and will lose you money.

- **Review margins.** Scrutinise margins in all areas of your business and increase or decrease the level of sub-contract, as appropriate.

- **Set a schedule.** Treat the next 12 months as if it was your last year before exit, develop an action plan and concentrate on filling the bottom line. If your exit is more likely to be two or three years down the line, take a view on your sales strategy, but still get into the mindset of a 12 month countdown.

- **Make sure your house is in order.** Take steps to resolve and reduce any liabilities from any outstanding legal disputes or anything else that may put off a potential buyer. Companies want to buy thriving businesses, not ones with baggage.

- **Hold regular exit reviews.** There is little point doing all of this and then forgetting about it while you get on with the day job. Go through the list on a regular basis, make sure all the steps are being followed and the benefits delivered.

- **SESF.** Keep everything simple, easy and straightforward (SESF). Never add complexity into the business and do not allow others to do so either.

None of the above points should stop you doing the right thing for your business today. But whatever move you make should always be done with one eye on the exit.

Exiting a business and taking your money is not a game of chance. Arguably it is the most important thing a fortune hunter does. Planning and thinking ahead means you can stay in control and realise the best value for your hard work.

Good luck.

Cut through the crap

Scribble your stuff here

www.diaryofafortunehunter.com
Follow me on twitter@lyndonx

Week 49

Upside down and inside out
(Focus on an exit - Part Two)

Having a 360 degree commercial view of your business is critical and crucial, and never more so than when you are considering your exit. But, you should not be alone in this endeavour. Although it is prudent, even necessary, not to alert employees that you are considering putting the company on the blocks, it is vital that they are on board to maximise every opportunity and get your firm into the best possible shape.

A commercial view means that everyone is making decisions, both strategic and operational, that benefits the business bottom line and set the foundations for the future.

Now, more than ever, is the time for everyone to stop chugging along and accepting that they are making a nice living from your firm. That would reduce it to the ranks of a 'lifestyle' business and that is not what you wanted to create when you set out to make your fortune.

The businesses that fail to realise their true value are the ones that lacked enough effort or understanding of where and who they are.

As a fortune hunter, you have to get everyone on board to help you towards your goal of a sale. To get everyone pulling in the right direction, I suggest a thorough inside out and upside down review of the business at the earliest opportunity.

If you have been following the strategies in this book, it will not be a shock to your team that you are reading them the riot act and tightening up on processes. They will be used to you putting them under pressure.

The aspects of the business that I would ask them to review are:

1. Speed of delivery - Is everything being done with optimum efficiency?

2. Time-wasting - Are members of the team perpetually using delaying tactics such as asking silly or irrelevant questions instead of getting on with the job in hand? Do they have a sense of urgency when it really matters?

3. Overmanning - Is the team's solution to problems to simply employ more people? Is there a better, less wasteful way? Wouldn't they be better off using their initiative?

4.   Industry trends - Are they all keeping up? An all-round lack of commercial awareness hinders and affects decision-making.

5.   Strategic thinking - Do they always leave it up to someone else? Have they adopted the mentality that anything tricky is "someone else's problem"?

6.   Short term thinking - Do they work from day-to-day, rather than towards the strategic vision?

7.   Strategic vision - Do they really understand what they are doing and why they are doing it? Even if they do, are they routinely driving projects through to execution?

8.   Attention to detail - Are they seeing an issue (or several issues) and ignoring it? Has the default position become that this is simply "the way it is"?

9.   Financial awareness - Are they leaving budgeting and the number stuff up to the accounts office?

10.   Financial planning - See above.

This is, of course, all about keeping your eye on the ball and making sure your team is helping you to put the business on the best possible footing. If there are gaps in any of these areas, it will only serve to give your would-be buyer additional negotiating power to lower their offer.

Remember, your focus at this time is to prepare and improve your business in order to maximise its total value. If you have reached any size, you will not be able to do this alone. Your senior team, in particular, should all have enough experience behind them and knowledge to pull together and create a plan to establish the profit you need for the valuation you desire. They are all accountable and responsible for the entire business; they have the title and they have the salaries, now they have to deliver.

This does not and should not mean that this is a cue for endless top-level meetings to discuss strategy going forward and how to rally the troops. Personally, I have always dubbed board meetings "boring meetings" because they add no value, sap our energy and steal our time. At least nine out of ten are useless and pointless and add nothing to the business. In short, they are a complete waste of time and, as I have emphasised so many times in this diary, time is money.

No, what we are looking for here is a bit of initiative. The idea of the review is to give the team a mild rocket, to get them focused on the task ahead (even if they are not fully cognisant of the true scope of the task). In an ideal world, they will hopefully be doing all these things already, but if they are not, the best outcome is that they will be reignited in their passion for the business and motivated for the push forward.

I want to be surrounded by people who care and have a passion for the business, not ones that are prepared to ignore risks and let opportunities pass them by. I do not expect everyone to be entirely strategic (although that would be nice), but I do require potential risks to be raised at every opportunity and questions to be asked as to what are we doing about them. Better still, I'd like people to come to me with solutions.

Selling a business is not far different from selling a house. If you want to get the best price, you need to tidy up and get your house in order and keeping it in order as a normal day-to-day part of building your business.

Can you do another draft of this? There's still a
couple of sentences people might actually understand...

Scribble your stuff here

Week 50

Squeeze the Juice

New investment =
ROI at some point v Attend to core business =
Instant growth

For many years, while on the quest for my fortune, I did everything I could to grow fast. I spent a fortune on new ventures, splashed out on marketing initiatives and set up new divisions left, right and centre. In fact, I did pretty much everything possible to increase my profit.

Except one thing.

Sadly, it turned out that I had missed the most important strategy I should have adopted from the start. I should have devoted my energies to squeezing every last drop of juice out of my core business before I started looking elsewhere.

Belatedly, a few years back with a view to an eventual sale, I turned my attentions to getting everything I could out of my existing business. My mantra became that we would do everything we did, only much, much better. Guess what? By tightening up processes here, changing a system there, and redirecting my energies to over here, I found £250,000 of savings. In a year! Yes folks, that is like finding a quarter of a million pounds hidden down the back of the corporate sofa. What a coup.

It wasn't that hard to find either. I'll give you an example. In my business, we buy data and ring it to death to get the most value out of it. At least, that is what I thought we were doing, but we weren't. While we were making a tidy profit we didn't ever really scrutinise whether we were getting the absolute maximum value from the data; we simply bought some more.

One of the pieces of data we collect is the renewal dates for commercial van insurance. Thus, when we have this data and know the policy is up for renewal, we will call the van operator and remind him it is just about to expire and offer to sort it all out for him. So far, so good, and clearly having a comprehensive source of data is key to all of this.

A few years back, if I asked my team about how they generated these dates, they would have assured me that, on average, they rang one and a half times per potential client in order to secure a record for this database.

It all sounded great on paper, particularly when it's said with a confident look, but it didn't mean anything. As it happened, the correct statistic should have been that an operator has to call four times on average to generate this lead. This is because the number may be engaged on the first time, the answer phone may be on and so on.

The point of explaining this in this level of detail is to show that no one (including me) had bothered to drill down into the nitty-gritty before. Just because someone had at some point come up with this magical one and a half times figure, no one had ever questioned it. My operators were religiously calling potential leads an average of one and a half times, when really they should have been doing it four times to maximise the potential of the data.

There are loads of things like this going on in every company, all the time. It takes analysis to pinpoint the potential weak areas, but once you do the rewards will be worth many times the effort you have expended.

After I did it and saw the returns, I couldn't believe it took me the best part of two decades to get around to it. It needn't take you this long to find the magic of squeezing the juice though because, thanks to my experience, I have worked out the golden rules of getting the most out of your business. It doesn't matter what industry you are in; some, if not all, of these tips will be relevant:

- Identify, through data, all of the statistics you can get your hands on in your business. If you are a retailer selling tins of beans, these statistics are the foundation to work out how you can sell more beans, without adding to the fixed costs. They are the starting point towards a little more creative thought.

- Review your product range. Which products are the easiest to sell to customers and which ones return you the most profit? Whilst reviewing products, ask yourself if there are any new products you could sell to your customers without the requirement to recruit more staff.

- If applicable, segment your data into categories such as highest converting, lowest converting, highest earning and lowest earning. Then focus on the highest converting, highest earning segments. It may also help to further break down the data into existing customers and new prospects.

- Look at the team and spot the 'maintainers'. These are the folks who resolutely do what they have always done and steadfastly maintain a level of activity and income that has been present for years. Have an informal conversation to explain that you are looking to up the pace and indicate areas they may like to improve. If the sluggish performance continues you will have to review the whole area of team activity. (More comprehensive advice on this is given in weeks 14 to 18)

- Examine your charging structure. In my own business model there are policy charges, but there is also the opportunity to charge for extras. For instance, in the past, when a customer lost their documents, we had always sent out replacements for free. Now we have added an administration charge of £25. Similarly, by following the example of my competitors, we began charging a 'new business fee' of £10 per policy to cover the administration costs of the paperwork for new clients. We were not adding to the wage bill and we still remained competitive; we were simply charging the customer a little extra to cover our true cost of issuing documents. That extra few pounds per item, when scaled up by thousands of clients, can make a huge difference to profits.

- If you can see that you have overdone your price hike and customer numbers begin to drop, be prepared to adjust the charges back. However, look carefully at the numbers before you completely reverse your decisions. If you are writing 1,000 new policies a month and all of a sudden you are writing 500 after putting on additional charges of £10, then that is no good. Yet, if you only lose 100 customers following the increased charges, it may still have worked to your advantage because you will be earning a lot more with a charge on 900 policies, than you were with no charge on 1,000 policies. The calculation varies according to your business, but the principle is still there, to earn more for doing less.

If you are making a profit, there is a tendency to become complacent. You miss things because you fall into the trap of doing what you have always done because it all seems to be going pretty well.

Although any or all of these steps could increase your bottom line profit by as much as 20 per cent or more, and none of them are particularly time-consuming. They simply require focus, planning and then execution. You'd be a fool not to try it.

Scribble your stuff here

Week 51

Exit mistakes to avoid

It is a common misconception among entrepreneurs that having started a company, built it up and conquered their sector, they are the best person to sell their business. They are not. In fact, attempting to sell your own business could well erode a huge part of the value a fortune hunter has strived so hard to get.

Selling a company requires skills and knowledge well beyond that of any entrepreneur. That is not an insult. It is the plain, unvarnished truth. You just don't know what you don't know. Selling a company for maximum returns requires an expert.

Swallow your pride and ask someone who sells companies for a living. A decent broker will add at least 10-12 per cent to the sales price and they'll help you get there faster, cleaner and with less hassle.

It doesn't mean you won't be in control. If you make it clear you won't accept a penny less than, say, £12 million and they get that price for you, you probably wouldn't begrudge paying 10 per cent for their services (Hypothetically, fees are normally a lot lower but this is to simply demonstrate my point). It would be money well spent.

You should, however, ensure that you choose the right expert. There is little point giving the job to the first person you meet, or the one that offers you the highest price tag. Approach it just like you would any other business challenge. Look at the facts, weigh up the options, listen to your instincts and make a wise decision. If you get the wrong broker, you could waste months and may even have to start all over again.

It's really important to get things right from the start. It is with this in mind that I have listed the 10 most common mistakes business sellers make - and how to avoid them:

1. **Failure to plan.**
   No one should wake up one day and decide to sell their business. They should be planning for months, if not years, ahead. Once you have made that decision, you should be constantly shaping your firm for a sale (for tips, see Week 48: Focus on an exit) and not wasting any cash. Similarly, you should have taken time to understand exactly what is involved in the sale process. Until you have covered these aspects, you will not be able to formulate a firm plan of what you want to achieve.

2. **Insufficient motivation to sell.**
   Following on from the above; do you really want to sell? It is odds-on that the buyer will want to know your reasons and will ask. Common reasons for selling include capitalisation, ill health or a career change. These reasons are all valid - what is important is that you have thought through your motivations and are 100 per cent behind the process.

3. **Asking for too much.**
   Any business is only ever worth as much as someone is prepared to pay for it. However, many people start out with completely unrealistic aspirations of the price they can get for their firm. Result? Disappointment. If your price is too high, no one will take you seriously and probably won't even ask for more information. This is why an expert is so important, but be wary of brokers who offer you a massive valuation because they may just be after your business. It helps to have a good knowledge of what other companies have gone for in the sector. It is also important to be realistic.

4. **…Or too little.**
By the same token, be wary of undervaluing the fruits of your hard labour. Sometimes, after years of hard work, business owners price their business too low because they are quite simply burned out and not thinking straight. Again, a good advisor with knowledge of the market will help here. Don't miss out on the payday for all your endeavours.

5. **Know your business.**
Nothing kills a deal quicker than lack of accurate information about numbers, suppliers, systems and clients. A potential acquirer is going to, quite rightly, dig deep into the detail. Make sure you have up-to-date figures and statistics on everyone and everything. Check and recheck these figures throughout the sales process in case anything changes.

6. **Misrepresentation.**
Yes, you want to get the best possible price. However, there is a big difference between getting the best possible price and misrepresenting your firm to prospective buyers. If you know your numbers (see above) there is no excuse. Don't be tempted to exaggerate, distort projections or cover up problems. It could jeopardise the sale, or lead to legal action at a later date.

7. **Underestimating the time involved.**
First time sellers consistently underestimate the time, effort, energy and sheer hassle involved in selling a business. It can take months of negotiations and nitpicking to do a deal. Unless you are emotionally and physically prepared for it, the strain can easily cloud your judgement. It could even erode your ability to run your business smoothly. Be prepared for the long haul.

8. **Doing nothing!**

Appointing a broker is not the end of your job. After all, no one has a greater knowledge about your business or a bigger motivation to sell than you do. You still need to constantly promote your business and make it saleable. Obviously, you don't want to make a big deal about the fact there is a 'for sale' sign over the firm, but the trick is to keep your firm in front of potential buyers all the time. Look at ways of creating a buzz around your company to get everyone talking about you. (For tips, look at Week 24 - Let's do PR!)

9. **Beware of tyre kickers!**

In any sales process, there will be a fair smattering of tyre kickers and time-wasters. Don't ever be afraid to ask for financial information or to do company checks. A serious buyer will expect this. Otherwise you will waste time and money by getting distracted by the wrong prospects.

10. **Failure to think about what happens next.**

Don't get so focused on selling your firm that you forget to think about what comes next. Some buyers will want the owner to stay on for a specified period to smooth the transition, while others prefer a clean break. Either is fine, as long as you have reached a mutually acceptable agreement during negotiations.

Employ an expert and keep these 10 tips in mind if you want to maximise your chance of success.

Remember the people buying your business will always think they can do a better job than you, so let them continue on that thought process. Maybe they can, maybe they can't; as long as you get your exit is what counts.

Scribble your stuff here

Week 52

Should you tell employees you are selling up?

You've always had an open door policy and encouraged your staff to come to you with any of their concerns. It's worked well. You've got a close-knit, happy team, who talk openly and share their problems before they become real issues.

So, what happens when your company is on the blocks? Inevitably, your door will be increasingly shut as you discuss confidential numbers around a possible deal. Your team may even see a steady stream of suited advisors walking in and out. They could hear worrying rumours on the industry grapevine.

Do you gather them all in a room and tell them you are preparing for an exit and expand with everything you know? Or, do you keep quiet and get on with the job in hand? My advice is, quite emphatically, keep your counsel.

There are a number of reasons for this;

1. If you are open about grooming the company for a sale and then nothing happens within 12 months, the team will become confused, frustrated and angry.

2. The continuing fear of the unknown will affect your firm's productivity - right at a time when you want everything and everyone to be firing on all cylinders.

3. Your best employees could well brush up their CVs and move on, in case they are caught in any later crossfire when/if the acquirer decides to change things.

4. Employees may have strong opinions about potential buyers and could even try to sabotage your plans if they are not happy with the way the process is going.

5. Employees could start gossiping to customers who could then become concerned that they will not get the same level of service or high quality product in the future. Your valued customers may even defect to your competitors, which will slow your business down and make it less saleable.

6.   The process will be stressful enough without having to consider how the team is going to react to every hiccup along the way.

The problem is, any halfway intelligent individual is going to sense something is up, even if you didn't have an open door policy. Once a sale is on the cards, the rumours will start to fly and you can't ignore this.

In the first instance, I would adopt a policy that holds off the inevitable rumours for as long as possible. In my company, for example, we have always been very aggressive on sales. We always want more! Everyone is aware of that and the pressure is always on for double digit growth. Companies that are not like this, and which are usually more accepting of the status quo, will stick out like a sore thumb when they enter the sales phase. All of a sudden, they'll be doing everything to maximise their figures and putting pressure on everyone to drive up the numbers. Anyone with a pulse is going to notice that something is afoot.

Then, as the process begins, I would craft a cover story. Send out the message that the company is working on getting some new financing because a fresh infusion of capital is needed to drive new growth. Alternatively, you could explain that you are on the lookout for acquisitions. Both these options require everyone's input to grow the business and fill the profit line.

You'll not be lying either. No sales process is certain. A lot of things could happen along the way and your dead cert prospect could fail to come through. If this does happen, it is quite probable that your Plan B will be to hold on to the company and keep growing profits, before returning to the marketplace another time. That means your staff should be concentrating their efforts on growth.

I would also consider setting up a 'war room' in an offsite office, or conference room, where potential buyers could go through the figures unobserved.

You will, of course, have to share the whole truth with key members of your senior team and do so well before you start looking for buyers. They need to be fully on board with what is going on because they will be part of the team that will be selling the business with you. However, don't sit down with this handpicked team until you have the answers to the following questions:

- What is in it for them?

- Can they compete to buy the company?

The first question can be quite a tough call. You need to come up with a percentage stake in the process, which will not only keep them engaged and motivated, but also as enthusiastic as possible. It also needs to be enough to encourage them to stick around and undertake all the extra hassle involved, because losing members of your top team can damage negotiations. You'll have to weigh this up against your desire to realise as much of your fortune as you can, after your years of hard work.

As for the second question, your choice here lies between giving your top team a shot which may keep them motivated and accepting that they could become a competitor in the bidding. If they are devoting their energies to competing to buy your company, it could lead to conflicts with other buyers and will clearly distract them from helping you with the process.

Finally, I would always be prepared for the news of a deal to leak. There is a high probability that it will happen somewhere along the line. The only way to manage this is to make plans ahead of time with this certainty in mind. I would draft an internal memo to all employees with the facts of the deal (that you can disclose) and the major talking points.

You won't need this document until the news leaks, but when it does, you will be able to move quickly to manage the news outflow in a calm and controlled manner. This is far better than reacting in a panic and rushing out a memo. That's how mistakes are made.

Selling a company is a stressful, time-consuming and an often fraught process, but you need to remember that it affects your employees too. No plan of how to manage the news will be perfect, but the important thing is you do have a plan and have anticipated some of the questions you can, and probably will, be asked. Just be honest with them at the right time.

Summary

Selling a business is usually a complex, time consuming and emotional experience but, like everything else in this book, it is a lot easier if you are prepared and aware of the potential pitfalls. Deciding to exit a business and then selling it is not something that will happen overnight though. You should be planning it well in advance and that means changing the way you run your business to tighten up on costs, identifying potential problem areas and making sure everything is in order. There is also a need to keep your team on board and motivated, because their continuing good efforts are vital to your success. Just as starting and running a company is not an easy path to take, selling it will stretch you to your limits. However, if you plan well, the reward will be worthwhile.

Afterword

It would be nice, at this stage in the diary, to round it all off by giving you a bullet point guide to sure-fire success as an entrepreneur. A week-by-week plan to get your business really rocking to make the millions you desire would be really handy.

However, just as every individual is unique, so is every business opportunity. Your path towards your millions will be different from everyone else's. What I have tried to do here is to set out some clues to what I believe will help you on the way. Some entries will be more applicable to you than others, and others will hopefully come in handy at different times in your journey to be a multi-millionaire. None of it will work though without your courage, determination and commitment to the cause.

It won't always be easy. In fact, it rarely will. Running a business will constantly challenge, frustrate and madden you. I guarantee it. What you have to remember (all the time) is that every success story starts with a big dream. I'm guessing your big dream is to make your fortune, which is why you picked up this book. You must never lose sight of that vision. When things get tough, it is what will sustain and drive you on.

You will find it a big help if you actively visualise success. What, for example, would it feel like to multiply your current income by five, or even ten times? How would your life change if you were a millionaire or multi-millionaire? What would your friends and former colleagues say if your business became the biggest in its field?

Never underestimate the power of having a bold vision and sticking to it doggedly. If you think every waking hour that you are going to be rich and successful, then you most likely will be. The more you believe in your goals, the more rapidly you will attain them. Sometimes that will mean that you need to take a risk or two, but, as they always say, "No guts, no glory."

If you are passionate about succeeding in your quest, you will change your life. After all, if you are doing something that interests you, it follows that you will give it your all and that is what will make it happen. Succeeding in business is all about hard work and you will only be able to put in the hours if you are crazy about what you want to achieve and even crazier about your business. No half measures will do.

I won't kid you. It won't be easy. You will have to work 60 plus hours a week in the early days in your strategy to be a multi-millionaire. You can kiss goodbye to after-office drinks every day, or regular weekends away with the family. Turning off your phone after 6pm, or ignoring emails until Monday morning is for losers. You will have to breathe, eat and drink your business. No one achieves big money unless they work hard. All the time.

One of the most important qualities you need is to be willing to learn. You don't need a string of professional qualifications (I certainly don't!), but I know my ability to constantly ask questions and be curious about everything has improved my position considerably. I've never worried about making a nuisance of myself and nor should you. A thirst for knowledge is important, and now more than ever with the rapid changes in technology. Find the right new development to spur your enterprise on and you could increase your chances of success exponentially.

Similarly, you won't ever be able to do it all alone. Make good contacts and stay in constant touch and recruit the absolute best people you can find to help you on your quest. Form alliances with clever, well-connected people who can help you and always be willing to help them in return.

Something else you need to consider as a fellow fortune hunter is that you may not always be the most popular person in the room. A touch of ruthlessness is a prerequisite, as far as I am concerned, and if you are always consumed by the need to be liked, then you may struggle here. Yes, you can and should be friendly to the people around you. They are, after all, the ones who will help you reach your goal. However, you also need to win some respect and be able to be firm to get things done the way you like and need to build your business. Tied in with this is the absolute necessity that you manage your time properly. There is little point working 12 or 15-hour days and driving yourself to near exhaustion, if a lot of your tasks could be completed more efficiently (or dispensed with altogether). There is nothing more guaranteed to sap your energy and resolve, than realising you've fluffed a big deal because you were too busy on something that really didn't need your attention.

The most important lesson you can learn as an entrepreneur is that an idea is only ever an idea until you make it happen. You may well dream of the millionaire lifestyle, but until you get off your butt and do something about it, it will only ever be a dream. The longer you pontificate, and waste time preparing and researching, the less likely it is to ever happen.

If you want to be a fortune hunter, get out there now and start the chase. It will be hard work and challenging, but it will also be the most exciting journey you ever take. There is nothing better than discovering your true potential and realising your dream.

What are you waiting for?

Good luck!